Paranormal Pursuits

Haunted Investigations, History, and Humor

Bryan "Ian Xavier" Dorn

Order this book online at www.trafford.com
or email orders@trafford.com

Most Trafford titles are also available at major online book retailers.

Printed in the United States of America.

ISBN: 978-1-4269-6604-0 (sc)
ISBN: 978-1-4269-6605-7 (e)

Trafford rev. 04/26/2011

www.trafford.com

North America & international
toll-free: 1 888 232 4444 (USA & Canada)
phone: 250 383 6864 ♦ fax: 812 355 4082

This book is dedicated to:

My mom Raenell, dad Harvey, brother Chris, and sister in law Laurel. Thank you for supporting me in my pursuit of ghosts and the making of this book.

Sarah, Mark, Derek, and the rest of BPIMN. You are the best group a guy could ask for. Without you, none of this could be possible.

To everyone else in the paranormal field. Whether you investigate or just a fan of the paranormal, keep up the fight. We are all in this together.

Introduction

Have you ever heard those strange footsteps in your house when you're all alone? Have you ever seen something move out of the corner of your eye? Have you ever placed something down in a certain spot, only to find it in another place? Ever get that feeling that you're being watched? If you have answered yes to these questions, don't worry, you're not alone.

Everyday, there are hundreds or even thousands of these reports told. The majority of people who report these claims are everyday people like you and me. They are hard working, level headed people who are just minding their own business. So, why are these people seeing or hearing these things? They all must be crazy right? Don't be so quick to judge.

Reports of ghosts and the paranormal have been spoken of for centuries. Ghosts are not just localized to one culture. They are spotted all over the world. Castles in England and Europe, fields in Africa, small farm houses in the Midwest and all the way to the White House. No matter where you go, people have a ghost story to tell.

So, what is a ghost? Well if we are to believe Hollywood, it's a see through figure, glowing white, and maybe clanking some chains. Whose only purpose is to give you a good scare, but not hurt anyone. However, most of the real ghost experiences are far more terrifying and harmful than most can imagine. I have yet to encounter this type, but look forward to the day when it happens.

My name is Bryan M. Dorn. I am a paranormal investigator from the state of Minnesota. I am the Director and Lead Investigator for the Bureau of Paranormal Investigation Minnesota Division (BPIMN). I have been interested in and studied the paranormal since I was 17 years old. When I was young, I used to be scared of ghosts, but as I got older, the stories intrigued me and I wanted to find answers. As they say, every story has some kind of truth to it.

Throughout this book, I will take you through some of my experiences and investigations in the paranormal. I will dwell on some of the paranormal history of a few places that I have investigated. I will also give you some personal stories, funny stories, and some tips if you wish to start your own company. I hope you enjoy.

CHAPTER 1: THE BEGINNING

I was born on November 21ˢᵗ, 1975 in New Prague, MN. My family lived in a small farming (even though we weren't farmers) community called Heidelberg. This was a place where everyone knew everyone. I did have some form of paranormal experience while living in Heidelberg, but more on that later. I am going to start by telling you about my grandma Dorn's ghosts.

Grandma Dorn lived in this small, cramped house on the main intersection in New Prague. It is considered cramped for me today, but when I was little, it was quite roomy. The house itself used to be a soda shop. I can remember grandma having the candy counter still stocked with candy. She would give me some whenever I would ask for it. That's really the only memory I have of her. In December of 1977, grandma Dorn passed away. I was 2 years old at the time and was not told of her death. My parents didn't know how to tell me so they just said that she went away for a while.

Over the next few months after her death, my mom and dad would clean up the house in order to get it ready for sale. Ownership of the house fell to my dad since he was the only one of her kids who was still in the state. My mom and dad would bring with while they were cleaning. I would just sit in the living room area playing with my toys and keeping to myself. According to my parents, I would get up for time to time and go to the staircase that lead up to the second floor. I would stand at the bottom of the stairs and just look up.

Mom would come over to me and ask me what I was doing. I would respond "watching grandma". Of course, when mom would look up, she would see nothing.

This continued for a few days and was now beginning to spook my mother a bit. Mom would tell me that "grandma wasn't here anymore". I would then tell her "but I hear her upstairs walking". Mom then told me to let her know the next time I see her. It was about an hour later when I walked over to the staircase again. I would never go up the stairs, just stand and look. Mom came over to me and asked me if I saw her. I said yes and described the bluish purple dress that they found her in. She died in the upstairs bedroom. This really made mom a little uneasy.

I would tell my mom that grandma would stand at the top of the stairs and smile at me. To me, remember I was 2 at the time, grandma was real and upstairs. I was never scared of the experience, it was grandma. Looking back on it now, it is possible that she was hanging around to make sure the house was presentable for sale. However, I have to ask myself this question. Was it real? Did I really see grandma? If I didn't, why was I able to describe what she was wearing? Like I said before, I don't have any real memories of her. I know she loved all of us grandkids and maybe she just wanted to see me one last time.

As time went on, I would see her less and less. By the time I was 4, I stopped seeing her all together. The house stayed in the family for years until it was sold in the early 1990's. If you ever are driving through New Prague, take a trip to the intersection of 19 and 21. Look for the house across the street from the gas station. Brown and tan brick house. That is the house where I had my first experience.

Like I said earlier, I do not remember any of these events. They are things my mom told me. Just like the next one of my "friend" Billy. Billy was my imaginary friend. That seems normal for a 3 year old boy right? For the most part, yes, but to my mom it was all too real.

One day, I was playing in the toy room in the Heidelberg house, when my mom heard me talking to someone. Mom came into the room expecting to see the window open and me talking to the neighbor. Not the case. I was sitting on the floor playing with some toy cars. She would then ask me who I was talking to. I would look at her and say "Billy". She thought it was cute at first, but got a little freaked as it went on.

As my mom went back to doing whatever see was doing, she heard me talking again. I would ask Billy a question, pause as if I was listening to a response, and then laugh at what his response was. I would roll one of my cars to Billy and ask him to roll it back. According to my mom, she heard the car roll back. She would hurry into the room to see me sitting in the same spot. I would look at her as though nothing out of the ordinary happened.

Billy and I did everything together. I would be playing with a ball in the backyard, when I threw the ball to Billy. But, Billy would never throw the ball back to me. I would cry (as a kid would do) and complain to mom that Billy wouldn't give me the ball back. My mom didn't know what to think. She asked me where Billy was and I would point to where the ball was sitting. So, mom would tell me to go and get the ball myself. So I would stomp over (again like kids do) to get the ball. I would reach down to pick it up then pull my hand back saying that Billy slapped it. Then mom would come outside and yell at Billy to play nice. I think she did this to try and make me feel better. I believe she must have been worried about me mentally.

Billy would only visit me and play with me at my house in Heidelberg. When I would go to the neighbors, grandma's (mom's side), or anywhere else, he would not follow. Mom said that she remembers on day that we were going to grandma's house for a family gathering. She asked me if Billy wanted to come with. She said that I went into the toy room to ask him. When I came out of the room, I said "Billy says that he has to stay here". Mom did find it odd that Billy would only stay in the toy room. When I returned from grandmas, Billy wouldn't play with me. I would go outside to play and Billy would only stare at me from the window. Over the next few years, Billy would disappear from time to time. I would only see him a few times a month. I would ask him where he went, and he would just say "home".

When I was 6 years old, one of the neighbors who we were very close to, passed away. This was my first real experience with death. I was finally told what it meant. Even though I was confused as to why, I did understand. I find it ironic now, but after the neighbor died, Billy disappeared for good. Did my experience with death send Billy away? If so, did he know he was a ghost and left because he didn't want me finding out? Improbable? Yes I do agree with you. However, it is the only explanation I have right now.

You can't say that it was just my imagination that created Billy. If you want to think that then fine, but you need to ask this. How do you prove it was my imagination? Most adults will say "Well if I didn't see it, then it didn't happen". Ok, then prove it wasn't there. These are some of the things that we can help prove or disprove while on an investigation. Some things however, can't be explained.

The whole Billy thing does give a little more credence to a theory that I have. Maybe, kids aren't talking to an imaginary friend. Maybe it is possible that they are talking to a ghost. One way to gather proof, is to set up an audio recorder in the room of a child when they are talking to themselves. This is a technique called Electronic Voice Phenomena (EVP). I will explain what that is in another chapter. By the time you read this, I will hopefully find some proof that Billy existed. I will be going to the Heidelberg cemetery in hopes to find a gravestone for a kid named Billy. I will be looking for a kid around the ages of 4 or 5. I will have to get back to you on this one.

CHAPTER 2:
HIGH SCHOOL & 1ST CASE

After Billy went away, I didn't have any other experiences with the paranormal. As I was growing up and going through school, I was mainly concentrating on sports and girls (nothing has changed about that). Once in high school, I would hear fellow students talk about hearing footsteps in their homes, and seeing shadow people in their basement. Once again, my interest was peaked and I got back into the paranormal.

I would go to the school library to read books on the subject. The school library was, shall we say, limited on that kind of stuff. So I turned to a few of the television shows (Sightings and Unsolved Mysteries) for information on hauntings. I would record them and watch them over and over to learn what I could. I was trying to learn why people were experiencing these things and what could I do to help them. One day while I was in the library, I overheard some other students talking about a supposed haunted place in a neighboring town.

My family and I were living in New Prague at the time and the neighboring town is called Union Hill. Union Hill is one of those very small towns, where if you are driving through and sneezed, you missed it. The house in question was a small white farm house on the outskirts of the town. This house was not occupied, but the land around it was used for farming. The barn on the property was also used to house farming equipment. I talked to my friends Kevin, Ted, and Jim to see if they would come with me. They all agreed and we went to the house that Saturday night.

The claims of activity that the classmates told me were the typical claims. They said that they heard disembodied footsteps, seeing a shadow person in the upstairs, and smelling a foul odor. Word had spread throughout the school that we were heading out to do this. The four of us were prepared for some of the trouble makers to play pranks on us while we were there. We are thankful that no pranks were played on us. We were all big guys and whoever would have played pranks would have gotten hurt.

I want to make one thing very clear right now. The way BPIMN conducts investigations is by getting permission by the clients first. We never trespass on private property. To go on property without permission, is stupid and could get you in trouble with the law. So remember if you want to start your own company, get permission. However, being 17 year old kids back then, we just walked onto the property. Fortunately for us, we did not get caught being there.

We started by entering the house through an open back door. We made our way past the small kitchen to the main living room. This place was a total mess. It looked like it was hit by a tornado (kind of like my bedroom). There were chairs and a couch turned over, 2x4 beams lying on the floor, nails all over the place, and broken glass. It was kind of unsafe to walk around. But, we were young, strong, and stupid so we found our way around.

As we were searching the living room, we came across a side door in the room. The door was open very slightly, so we were able to peak inside. It looked like some form of a den. I tried to push the door open, but it wouldn't budge. Jim and Ted gave it a go as well, but with the same result. So now Kevin, Ted, and I who were all over 250lbs, had to take two running starts at the door before we got it open. After we got in, we wanted to see what was keeping the door from opening. It turns out that there was a desk propped against the door. This made me think, "who propped the desk". How did they get out of the room? There was a small window in the room, but it was painted shut. This was a mystery to us.

We looked around the floor to see what we could find. The room was a mess just like the living room. More chairs turned over and papers scattered all over the floor. There was nothing really of interest in this room other than some of the papers were from the New Prague School Board of 1940. We sat in the room for about 20 minutes trying to get any spirits to make contact. After nothing happened, we left to go to the next area.

We decided to go back into the kitchen area. The whole time we were there we were looking for a ghost, but we were also looking for some cool things as well. Like the den, the kitchen didn't give us anything of interest either. There were some old food cans that looked like they were left over from the 1940's as well. We tried to get Jim to eat some of the food, but he declined. This was probably a very good move on his part.

While on the first floor, we tried to find the entrance to the basement. We checked all the doors, but could not find it. All of us were too big to squeeze through the small windows of the basement so we scrapped the idea. We then went to the staircase that lead to the upstairs. After inspecting the stairs, we saw that they were coming undone. We determined that it was unsafe for all of us to go to the second floor, so Jim and Ted stayed downstairs. Kevin and I went upstairs and noticed that there were many holes in the floor. We explored the three rooms upstairs and saw that they were unsafe to be in. No joke, about 70% of the bathroom had rotted away. This place should have been condemned.

We went back downstairs to try to make one last attempt to make contact with any spirits in the house. However, we did not have any excitement of the paranormal kind. We did have a small scare though. As we were asking for a sign of a ghost, we heard a truck driving up the driveway. We knew that we had to get out of the house fast. We stayed quiet as we watched the truck drive into the barn. Then the four of us ran as fast as we could. Looking back on it now, it must have looked funny watching these four large men trying to run fast in two feet of snow.

We got back into our cars and drove back to my house. We exchanged thoughts on what we did and all came up with the same conclusion. We all felt that the place was not haunted. The following Monday at school, the other students would come up to us and ask what we saw. We were honest and said nothing. The experience had me wondering something. Are there any other places around her that we could investigate? That's when I remembered this house in my old home of Heidelberg. This was a place I visited during the day when I was young, but would never go in. Now that I was older, I felt it was time. I talked to the guys again, and we made plans to go there in 3 weeks. From this point on, even though I didn't know it at the time, I became a paranormal investigator.

CHAPTER 3:
OLD MAN ZICKA'S PLACE

The place that we were going to investigate was another old, white farm house. This one was ironically and creepily located across form a cemetery. The house was known as the Old Zicka Place. Don't bother going to look for it, it was torn down in 1994 and a new house is located there. Being teenagers, we didn't have much for equipment. All we had with us were flashlights and our courage. Stupidity could be added there as well depending on how you look at it.

We arrived on a Saturday night around 11pm. We parked our cars down the dirt road from the house. They were parked by a few houses so it looked as though we were visiting them. The driveway leading up to the Zicka place was one that came out of a horror movie. It was a long, winding, dirt road that had grass growing over it. AT night, the house does give off a creepy feel, especially as you got closer to it. Joining me on the investigation were Ted and Kevin again. Also joining us was my other friend Brian. When we opened the front door and walked in, it did feel like a scary movie about to happen.

After going past the front porch, we entered the kitchen area. To our right, was the living room. In the living room were chairs that were covered with white sheets. I kid you not, white sheets. If that doesn't scream horror movie, I do not know what does. We investigated the living room by asking whatever was there to make its presence known. We stayed in the living room for about 40 minutes without any action. So, we got up off a very comfortable couch, and moved to the kitchen.

The kitchen was very small and cramped. Not a lot of space for four big guys. We looked through some of the drawers and found some old pictures of people we didn't know. In an adjacent closet/pantry, we found some old medicine bottles and an old playboy magazine. It wasn't in very good condition or we would have taken it to see if it was worth any money. Hey we were kids, what do you think was going through our heads at that time. It was a cool find.

As the four of us were searching the kitchen, we all heard what sounded like footsteps coming from the upstairs. Now I thought to myself, it's time for some action. Ted and Brian stayed in the kitchen to look at the pictures (I'm sure they were looking at the playboy), while Kevin and I went to the staircase. Kevin and I stood at the bottom of the stair looking up hoping to see something. We didn't see anything, but the footsteps started getting louder. It was like someone was walking towards the top of the stairs. I shined my flashlight up the stair to get a better look, but when I did that the footsteps stopped. Even though we were not experienced investigators, we were thinking about possible explanations for the footsteps. What it a raccoon or a cat? We were going to find out.

Kevin and I slowly walked up the stairs until we reached the top. We shined our flashlights around to see that the upstairs was just one big room. It seemed that this floor was the master bedroom. The bed was still there, a lot of old man Zicka's clothes were still on the floor, and some of his person things. Looking back on it, I wish I knew then what I know now. Now I know how to conduct an EVP session and how to work an Electromagnetic Field (EMF) meter. Back then I could just mimic what I saw on shows like *Sightings*. I finally said out loud, "Old Man Zicka, if you are here, come out and show yourself". I was 17 and stupid, get off me.

After asking multiple times without a response, Kevin and I went back down to the kitchen to meet up with the others. I remember asking Brian if he could hear us walking upstairs. Brian said, "We could hear you, but you guys walked too soft. The steps we heard were heavy boot steps". As we were discussing the sound, we all heard the boot steps again. The steps seemed to walk to the top of the staircase again. Why wouldn't it ever come down? I walked to the bottom of the stairs again, but still couldn't see anything. The footsteps were clear as day. After a few seconds of creepy silence, the footsteps walked away from the stairs. This was getting weird.

We decided to take a break from the house to investigate the two barns on the property. Before we left, we told whatever was there that we'd be back. The big barn was used to house the cows, horses, pigs, and other animals. The smaller of the barns had all the farm equipment. In the big barn, we didn't have any experiences. We did find two animal skeletons (one dog and one horse). Likewise, we didn't have any experiences in the small barn either. We did find a tractor that looked as though it hadn't been used in 30 years. We stood outside talking about things when we heard a crash come from inside the house. The four of us quickly ran back into the house to see what happened.

We got back into the house and searched the first floor. Nothing had crashed in the kitchen or living room, so we knew where we had to go. That's right, back upstairs. When we got upstairs, we noticed that a glass jar full of nails had exploded on the floor. Kevin and I remembered this jar being on a small dresser when we were up there last. What could have caused the jar to crash? Was it the wind? There was a small window that was open allowing in a small breeze. That being said, it is possible that it could have blown over. If that is the case, how did a small breeze make a glass jar move 15 feet? Plus the window was on the opposite side of the room. We do not have an explanation of how it happened.

It was around three in the morning, when we wanted to take a look in the basement. The only way in into the basement was to climb down a rope that was suspended from the porch ceiling. The staircase had had rotten and fallen to the basement floor. Well the four of us could have gotten down, but there was no way we could have gotten back up. We didn't feel like becoming permanent residents, so we scrapped the basement idea.

We went back into the house area to try to make contact one last time. We asked that if the footsteps we heard were Mr. Zicka's for him to do it again. We then heard the heavy boot steps one last time. After hearing the boot steps one last time, we felt that it was time to leave. As we were walking back to our cars, Brian had one last experience. We had walked about half way down the driveway when Brian had the urge to look back at the house. Brian said that he saw a green light floating in the top floor window. The rest of us didn't see it, but after we experienced that night, we believed him. The Old Zicka place was a great place to experience the paranormal. I was satisfied with what we had done, but it left me with more questions. I knew right then that I would want to do these investigations more often.

CHAPTER 4: TO THE EAST COAST

After graduating high school, I put paranormal investigation on hold to follow my dream. Ever since I was 8 years old, I wanted to be a professional wrestler. So 3 days after I received my diploma, I went to Minneapolis to be trained by the greatest trainer in wrestling, Eddie Sharkey. For the next 14 years (I am not retired by the way), I put ghost hunting on hold to concentrate on wrestling. While in locker rooms, I would hear other wrestlers tell stories of the strange and unusual. Most of the stories were stretched and false, but some were so good that they caught my attention. Hearing these got my paranormal juices (get your mind out of the gutter) flowing again.

In May of 2008, I took a two week break from wrestling to go on a paranormal road trip. I set up an investigation at a haunted asylum in New York on a Friday, but I left on Sunday. I took this trip for two reasons. First, I needed a break from wrestling and from my security job. Second, I knew that if I was going to put my name out there as an investigator, I would have to build a resume. So you ask, why the east coast? What better way to start then in the oldest part of the country.

I drove the entire way out there (26 hours total) while making a few stops. I had a friend of mine with me, so I was able to take breaks and nap a bit. I would like to make a side point now if I may. I tend to hear a lot of people say "we need to save the trees, our forests are dying". Well to those people, I have just one thing to say to them. MOVE TO PENNSYLVAINA! That's all I saw while driving through that state. Ok, I'm done with that.

As I was driving, I went through the states of New Jersey, New York, and Connecticut. I was driving through Stamford, CT when I saw the World Wrestling Entertainment office. I wanted so badly to stop in, and see if I could get a job. Unfortunately, it was more than likely the closest I will get to that building. I can say I saw it though. I had a lot of time to waste, so I decided to drive all the way to Rhode Island. Why there? Rhode Island is the home of The Atlantic Paranormal Society (TAPS). They are the group that is featured on the SyFy Channel. I have always wanted to meet them and here was my chance.

My friend and pulled into Warrick, RI around 6:30pm. We parked the car and walked to where I thought the TAPS office was. When we arrived to the site, it was a pottery store. We walked the town asking people where it was, and to our surprise, not many knew what we were talking about. We were both exhausted, so we found a hotel and crashed. We would try again in the morning when we were fresh.

The next morning, we looked up the address of the TAPS office on the internet. It turns out that they moved to the outskirts of the town. We checked out of the hotel and made our way to where they were. We drove down the street that the website had told us to go to. I drove up and down the street about six or seven time with no luck. The car was getting low on gas, so I pulled into a gas station to fill up. My friend went inside to use the little boy's room. As I stood pumping gas, I turned to look across the street. Take a wild guess as to what I saw. My friend came out of the gas station and asked me why I was laughing. I pointed across the street; he turned to look, and started laughing too. Why were we laughing? Across the street was the TAPS office. It was attached to the end of a small strip mall. We felt like fools.

We pulled up to the front doors of the building. I couldn't believe that I was here. The windows were all blacked out with TAPS written in yellow stencil. The TAPS trucks and van were parked outside. I walked up to the door and tried to open it, but it was locked. I could hear some people talking behind the door, so I think they were having a production meeting. SO, we snapped a few pictures and got back into the car. Even though I didn't get to meet them (then), it was cool to be at their headquarters. It is something that I will never forget.

CHAPTER 5: SALEM, MA PART 1

After leaving Rhode Island, we drove into Massachusetts. We wanted to do a little bit of sight seeing, so we headed to Boston. Let's start by saying that driving through Boston SUCKS! The roads are laid out in a grid like they are in Minneapolis. The streets in Boston zigzag all over the place. We wanted to check out the actual Cheers bar, but we couldn't find it. We used a GPS mapping system, but that was no use. It told us to make turns after we were three blocks past the turn. That GPS is currently sitting at the bottom of a river in Chicago. That's a funny story, I'll tell it later.

We got fed up with trying to maneuver through Boston, so we got back on the freeway and headed north. I did get to kind of see Fenway Park. We drove past it anyway. There's another sports stadium that I can cross of my list of things to see. As we were driving north, I had a great idea. Let's go to Salem. I asked my friend if he wanted to go, and he responded "hell yeah". Salem is famous for the witch trials of the 1600's. At first we were going there for some fun, it turned into a mini investigation.

We arrived in Salem around three in the afternoon. We found out that pedestrians don't watch where they are going in Salem. We almost ran over at least 30 people. There must be something about the east coast, driving there sucks. Anyway, we found a place to park and then walked to the information center. It was ironic that the first person we talked to there was a fellow Minnesotan. Her name was

Julie and she was from St. Paul. She said that she came to Salem for school and just fell in love with it. She was a tour expert and she recommended some point of interest to us.

We took the tours of some of the wax museums and got a history lesson about witches. Things like a male witch is just that a witch. Not a warlock like Hollywood likes to say. Even though, I like warlock better. We also learned where the witch riding a broomstick came from. Here is the story in short. While women were attending there gardens, they would use a broom to keep it clean. An old custom/ superstition was to jump over the broom forward and backward to ensure a good harvest. Well some of the easily fooled (jesus freak and religious type) would see a woman hovering over a broom. They then thought that the woman was using supernatural powers, and then they were labeled a witch. SO from then on, witches rode brooms. Bet you didn't know that did you? Its ok, neither did I before then.

We stopped at the shops in town to see what they were selling. Most of the places were selling different spices and herbs (not that kind). A few of the stores were selling gothic style clothing. I did buy a few t-shirts and a picture of a bat dressed as Batman for a friend of mine back home. After a little shopping, we walked to another store called Remembering Salem. It caught our eye due to the guy standing out in front of it. He was about in his late 30's or early 40's and dressed in colonial style clothing. His name was Dave and he worked at the shop with his girlfriend. They were very nice people.

Dave told us that he runs the walking ghost tours at night. I told him that we were paranormal investigators who were in the area to do a case later in the week. Dave said that he would be honored if some investigators would be on his tour. He spoke with his girlfriend (who I guess owned the place) and offered us spots on the tour for half price. We accepted and told him that we would be back for the tour at 10:30pm. Now half price wasn't free, but in this day and age, you take what you can get.

Since the tour was going to take us into the next morning, we decided to find a hotel. We drove to a nearby suburb of Salem and stayed at a Days Inn. The hotel was kind of run down, but it did have cool lobby and was staffed by this creepy looking, old dude. He looked as if was left over from the witch trial of the 1600's too. I know that it was bad to say that, but you didn't see this guy, we did.

After grabbing a late dinner, we drove back into Salem. We parked in the same parking lot and walked to Remembering Salem. The equipment we had with us was just a night vision video camera and a digital still shot camera. A group was already waiting outside the shop when we arrived. Dave went over a few ground rules for the tour before making a nice gesture. Dave told the rest of the group that we were paranormal investigators visiting from Minnesota. He told the group that if they had anything in their photos, that we'd be happy to look at them. Thanks Dave, that was very nice of you.

The first place on the tour was the Gardner-Pingree House. This is a two story house that dates back to the mid 1700's. One of the stories is that a murder happened in the house in the 1800's. After the murderer was caught, tried, and put to death, the murderer's house was moved next door to the victim's. I am not sure what they were thinking when they made that move. However, after the move was done, that's when the activity started. The claims of activity were seeing strange lights floating through the upper floors, shadows moving past windows, and hearing disembodied voices. We weren't allowed to go inside, so we just filmed and shot photos from the sidewalk. We did not capture anything out of the ordinary this time around. That last sentence should give you a clue of something will happen later.

As the tour went on, we visited some places that were cool but not much as far as paranormal history. The places were about some of the famous people who lived in the Salem area. Most of the buildings were over 300 years old. It is amazing how these buildings and homes have stood the test of time. One of the stops on the tour was The First Salem Church. This was a very small building with a iron fence all around it. Inside the fence were a bunch of gravestones. The gravestones were placed very close together. We were told that this was an actual gravesite of some of the witches who were tired. After seeing the size of the graveyard, if it's true, then these were very small people.

The next stop on the tour, was a large old prison. This building covered almost four city blocks. It was a spooky looking place complete with stepals, broken windows, and iron fencing. Some of the other people on the tour brought some of their pictures up to us to look at. Two of the people were these two Australian girls with smoking hot asses. They were Goth style and wore tight jeans and just looked yummy. Sorry, I got a little side tracked. We looked at their pictures, but had to break the bad news to them. We didn't see anything paranormal in them. The "orbs" that they caught were just bugs that were reflecting the light from the flash back into the camera. You could actually see the wings of the bug if you looked close enough. I felt really bad for the others in the group who we told the bad news to. Mainly for the Australian girls.

After the prison, we went to an open field. It was a small field that had a few houses around it. In the field was an area where grass refuses to grow. It is a little ironic, because this is the area where supposed witch Giles Cory was pressed to death on September 19th, 1692. Giles was accused of witchcraft by Ann Putnam, Mercy Lewis, and Abigail Williams. During the trial, Giles Cory refused to make any type of plea (guilty or not guilty). The reason he was accused of witchcraft, was because Mercy Lewis had a dream about him. She stated that his spirit was able to leave his body and torment her. She also claimed that his spirit wanted her to write a book called "The Devil's Book". Great evidence don't you think?

Since Giles wouldn't make a plea, the judge found him guilty. He was sentenced to be pressed until he confessed or he was dead. The townspeople took him out to the field, stripped him naked, and placed a board on him. The, they started to add heavy stones. Once in a while, the judge who was there would ask "What is your plea".

Giles would only respond with "More Weight!". After about an hour, Giles Cory was crushed to death. Not a very good way to go.

After hearing this story, a bunch of us took some pictures. Nothing showed up and I was getting a little annoyed. When Dave said that we needed to get to the next stop, I demanded that Mr. Cory show himself. I took one last picture at the spot of the crushing. Above the spot was a bright, perfect shaped orb. Now, I do not put much weight in orbs at all, but I find it weird that this one appeared when I asked for it. As of right now, I do not have an explanation for this.

The next stop on the tour was a small house that was next to the main witch cemetery. This house is called the Corwin Witch House. It's a small two level house that was built in the 1700's. It was remodeled a bit, but most of it's originality is still intact. This house is now used for the Salem Chamber of Commerce. The claims of paranormal activity are seeing a little girl in the second floor window. The girl is described as being about five or six years old, long brown hair, wearing a white dress with a black shall on her shoulders. Let me tell you that this one got me going. As people were snapping pictures, people were shouting and pointing at the window. I looked up myself and could not believe me eyes. I could swear I saw the little girl standing there. I shined my flashlight at the window, but whatever was there had gone. However, when the camera flashes started again, she was back in the window.

Did I really see the little girl? If I did, then why did it disappear when I shined my flashlight at the window? Also, why was she standing so still? If this did not happen, the how do you explain the fact that nine of us all saw the girl? Is it possible that we only saw her because of the story and it was in our minds? I suppose it if, but could all nine of us be in tune together? These are questions that were going through my head, and I wanted to find out the answers.

After calming ourselves down, it was over to the witch cemetery. This is where most of the witches and the judge (Judge Hawthorne) who tried them are buried. We didn't experience anything paranormal here, but it was a great part of history to be in. We finished the tour back at the Remembering Salem shop. We were standing around talking when Dave said that we could take a few last minute pictures of the Gardner-Pingree House. As we were shooting video, we saw something that we couldn't believe.

We were shooting our video at the lower level south side window. We zoomed in on what looked like a mirror. What we saw looking back at us was something else. In the mirror we saw a face. It was a bald head, pure white, with very dark, sunken eyes. As we stayed on it, it looked at us for a few seconds, and then looked down at the floor. Then it popped its head up and looked at us again. It seemed to give us a little smirk and then disappeared.

This was absolutely amazing. Did we just see a spirit face? That's what it looked like to us. If so, who was it? Why did it make eye contact with us? Was it trying to tell us something? If we did not see a face, then what was it? There was no one in the house at that time. We were able to rule out interference from outside street lights. What could it have been? This and the mystery of the little girl were things that I was going to find out the next day.

CHAPTER 6: SALEM PART 2

After the tour was over, I went over to a local bar to use the restroom and grab a soft drink. The place I went to was called the Lyceum Restaurant. This was a place that was featured on season three of *Ghost Hunters* on the SyFy channel. I sat down at the bar talked with some of the staff. After telling the staff that I was an investigator, they began to tell me of the activity that they had before I walked through the door. The lady behind the bar told me about some of the glasses moved by themselves on the bar. I was thinking to myself, how convenient that it stopped when I walked in.

As I sat there, I was remembering the Ghost Hunters (TAPS) episode. I remembered that TAPS did not catch any paranormal activity there. The only thing that happened to them at the Lyceum, was on the cash register printing receipt that read "good morning". When confronted by this, the bar owner told TAPS that the register does not print that out. Just before closing, the bar owner begged the spirits to perform for me, but it was to no avail. Did something really happen in this place before I walked in? I only have their word to go by. Like I said earlier, I find it strange that it stopped before I walked in. On the plus side, it was cool to be somewhere that TAPS investigated.

My buddy and then decided to call it a night and head back to the hotel with the creepy old guy. Before we fell asleep, we watched the video footage again. We were running through every explanation we could think of for that face we caught. None of them seemed to fit. We also examined the photos that we took. In one of them, you could see the little girl that was standing in the second floor window of the Corwin Witch House. We really needed to look at the building during the day. Same was true of the Gardner-Pingree house. In one of the lower floor windows, we saw what looks like a silhouette of a person looking at us. We agreed that we needed to dig deeper.

We woke up at ten in the morning and had breakfast. We packed up the car and made our way back into Salem. After we parked the car, we walked to the Remembering Salem Shop. We showed Dave and his girlfriend the video of the face. They were in awe that we actually caught something. We asked Dave what was in that room of the house. He said that he wasn't sure, but if we wanted to wait until 3pm, we could take the tour. Well, we had to be on the road by then, so we passed. Dave then took us to the back end of the Gardner-Pingree House. From a back door window, we could partly see into that room. The only thing we could see was a table that did have a small plant sitting on it.

Is it possible that the plant could have caused the face to appear? It is, but if you go that route, then you have to ask this question. How do you explain that the face looked at us, looked down to the floor, and then looked back at us? Remember that it also disappeared. If it was the plant, wouldn't the face have stayed in one place? There are so many questions in this line of work. Just after you have come up with an answer to a question, five questions take its place. As far as the face goes, we are labeling it as paranormal. That doesn't mean that it was a ghost, it just means that we don't have an explanation yet.

So what about the pictures of the little girl? Well, we feel we were able to come up with an explanation for those. During the day, we were able to see what the window looked like. Here is what we found. In the middle of the window, there is a small wooden post that goes up about ¾'s of the way. The glass of the window is made up of little brown and green diamond shapes. When the light hits the glass at the right angle, it does make the post look like a girls with a white dress and dark shall. We were able to recreate this multiple times. We went back to Remembering Salem and told them what we had found. To say they were a bit disappointed would be an understatement. They were glad that we were being true investigators and went to find the answers. They said that they were going to keep the stories in the tour. All the power to them.

Being in Salem was truly amazing. We got a history lesson, got to meet some cool people, met some hot Australian girls, and take a ghost tour that had some possible evidence. If you are ever lucky enough to go to Salem, spend as much time there as you can. Take in the sights, relive the history, and take the Remembering Salem ghost tour. We had a lot of fun and I know you will too.

CHAPTER 7:
HEADING FOR THE HILLS

We left Salem at 2:30pm that Wednesday afternoon. It was a long drive to Rochester, NY so we took turns driving stopping only for food and gas. We arrived in Rochester around 11pm that night. The hotel we stayed at that night was on the edge of the city by the railroad tracks. This scared us a bit because bad things happen by the railroad tracks. We weren't in our room twenty minutes when we heard an argument coming from the next room. It was a man and a woman arguing over money. We listened with glee as we found out as to why they were arguing. Apparently, the woman was a prostitute who got shafted (no pun intended) on her money. The guy still wanted his sex, but she wouldn't give it. She then got on the phone to call her pimp. After the call was over, she told the guy "you gonna get yo ass beat". We couldn't believe what we were hearing.

They guy started to apologize to the woman over and over. He must have been on his knees because she said "Oh get up you pussy". By this time we were laughing a bit loud. The woman must have heard us because she pounded on the wall and yelled "Shut up!". We did because we didn't want the pimp coming into our room too. Granted we are both tough guys, but we were strangers in a strange land. There wasn't anyone going to help us out. After 10 minutes, the pimp came into the guy's room. We assume that he paid up because they left the room laughing. You have to love New York.

The following day was our last relax day before the big investigation. After breakfast, we went to go see the movie *Ironman*. My friend had seen the movie already, so he was texting "friend" throughout the whole thing. When the movie was over, we did a little touring of Rochester. We stopped at a local bar and played darts for a while. That night we went a saw a Rochester Redwings baseball game. Before the trip, I had my mom use her baseball connections to set up two tickets. My friend doesn't like baseball, so he kept himself busy with beer and texting. I was trying to hit on this very good looking woman who was selling hotdogs. I think if I lived in Rochester it might have worked, but I do not.

The following morning (Friday), we made our way to East Bethany, NY. It was another long drive with nothing to see except for trees. There's another one for you tree hungers. We arrived in East Bethany around 2 in the afternoon. The place that we were investigating didn't open until nine that night, so we had a lot of time to waste. We decided to drive to the building so that way we knew where it was. The place was in the middle of nowhere (as most of these places are). After finding it, we cruised the town of East Bethany. This took about ten seconds of our time. There were no shops or anything. A place that time and technology forgot.

After looking at a map, we went to the nearest big city we could find. The city of Batavia was only about 12 miles away. We were hungry, so we stopped at a small local diner. The look on the faces of the other patrons was priceless. My friend and I were dressed in all black and both of us have lots of tattoos. They looked at us as if we were there to collect their souls. It was great.

We found a table in the back of the diner and sat down. For about 15 minutes, no one took their eyes off of us. Even the wait staff looked at us funny. They were probably drawing straws to see who had to wait on the two freaks. Eventually one of the waitresses came over to us. She was an older woman, but was good looking. She said hi to us and told us about their specials. We just ordered chicken and mashed potatoes. One of the other patrons got up the courage to ask us where we were from. Once we told them who we were and why we were there, the ghost stories came out of the woodwork. Just goes to show, that you can't judge a book by its cover. We are nice guys to talk to.

After lunch, we still had some time to waste. We grabbed the GPS and looked for anything to do. We looked up the nearest bowling alleys and saw that there was one only three blocks away from where we were. So, we were off to bowl a few games. There was just one problem. The place was closed for repairs. Just our luck. So, my friend and I looked at each other and asked "Well, now what?". We then remembered that we saw a minigolf course on the edge of town. My friend said, "Why don't we go there?". I looked at him and said "Ok, but don't be surprised if it's closed".

We pulled into the parking lot of the course and saw a few people on the driving range. O, this place was open and we could waste some time. Yeah, not so much. We went into the video arcade to play some games. About half of the games didn't work. We did play a few of the sport games that seemed to date back to the 1980's. We then moved to the minigolf course. The course was made all out of concrete, meaning no turf. The water hazard was a small kid's swimming pool. This thing was low tech to say the least.

Well, we made the best out of a poor situation. My friend beat me at concrete golf and we each spent about ten dollars on the few games that worked. We did get some rewards though. When the owner of the place wasn't looking, my friend and I helped ourselves to some of the "prizes" they had. These prizes are the types you see at arcades where you play games for tickets. We grabbed a few small rubber balls, some of those plastic spider rings, and some pencils. We didn't bother grabbing any of the candy. The candy looked as if it was there since 1920. We also took some golf balls from the driving range. After spending about two hours there, we still had five hours to waste.

Again, we turned to the GPS, and looked for a bowling alley. The GPS showed us that there was one in a neighboring town. We drove to this town and it was closed as well. We should have seen that one coming. So, we found a small bar and played darts again. This time we asked about the place we were investigating and one guy told us that he's seen strange lights in the windows when driving past it one night. On one else talked to us in that bar. They were either too shy to share a story or they just didn't want to talk to strangers. The time was now eight in the evening. So we grabbed some snacks at a local gas station and headed out to look for ghosts.

CHAPTER 8: ROLLING HILLS

We arrived at the place that this whole trip was based on. The place in question is known as Rolling Hills Asylum. This building was built in 1827. The property was used as a carriage house and a tavern back in the 1790's. Interesting fact, the carriage house still stands on the property to this day. After Rolling Hills opened its doors in 1827, it was used to house orphans, the criminally insane, paupers, unwed mothers, and anyone else who couldn't look after themselves.

It stayed that way until 1950 when it was used as a nursing home. It was then closed in 1972 after a new facility was built in Batavia. The building stood empty until 1992 when it was reopened as the Carriage Village Mall. People would rent rooms in the building and sell handmade crafts, dolls, and other things. It was abandoned again in 2002. In 2004, it was purchased by Lori Carlson and her husband. The Carlson's wanted to fix it up to what it looked like back in its early days. The renovations stopped when they started to experience odd things happen.

Lori would have her hair pulled by an unknown force. She would hear footsteps coming from the floor above when she knew she was alone in the building. She would also see shadow people move between the rooms. She got in touch with some local paranormal investigators and they came in to do an investigation. After getting constant evidence, the Carlson's opened up Rolling Hills to paranormal groups as a training building. In 2009, the Carlson's sold the building. The new owners, Jerry and Sharon Coyle, have once again opened the building to paranormal teams.

The doors opened at 9pm and we gathered in the main office. There were about twenty other people joining the investigation party. We were given the history of the place, the claims of paranormal activity, and then split into groups. My friend and I were teamed with a married couple. The wife was one of the most annoying people I have ever met, but more on that later. I will be taking you to each spot individually, talking about the paranormal claims, and telling you what we found and what we were able to explain.

The first area of interest was the third floor. This is where the director of the property back in the 1800's had his office. Other staff had offices and personal quarters up on the third floor too. Once the building became a nursing home, the director's office became the head doctor's office. The claims of activity up here were hearing the growling of a dog, and seeing a black dog with glowing red eyes. Well, the whole time we were up there, we did not hear the dog or see the dog. However, we did have two experiences on the third floor.

The first experience was a door that had closed on its own. We did not catch this on video, so it goes down as a personal experience. We were in the doctor's office looking around and asking questions. In the corner of the room, there was a closet that had its door wide open. I asked out loud, "If there is anyone here, could you please close the closet door?". It did not close while we were in there, but it did close. We had left the doctor's office to check out a different room, when we heard a noise come from behind us. When we went back into the doctor's office and saw the closet door closed. There was no breeze in the room or anyway we can see how the door closed. No explanation so we label it paranormal.

The second experience was also in the doctor's office. We were sitting in silence in the room to get a better feeling of things. After about ten minutes, we heard what sounded like footsteps coming down the hallway towards the doctor's office. Thinking that some of the other investigators were walking around, I went out to have a look. There was no one in the hall or even on the floor. I went back to sit down, when we started to hear the footsteps again. This time, they walked up to the doorway of the doctor's office and stopped. Was this a ghost from the past coming to see who was in the office? Don't know, but it was a cool experience.

The next stop was the second floor. This floor was separated into two wings, the west wing (men's ward) and east wing (women's ward). The claims of activity in both wings were hearing disembodied voices, seeing full body apparitions, and seeing objects move on their own. We searched the west wing for about an hour without any experiences. After deciding that we would come back later, we made our way to the east wing. When we arrived, there was a group of about ten people sitting at the end of a long hallway. Our legs were tired so we joined them. What happened next was not only strange, but hard to believe.

After I sat down, I asked some of the others as to what they were doing. One of the guys told me that they were watching a nurse waling in and out of some of the rooms. My friend and I looked at each other in disbelief, but stayed to see for ourselves. Then the wife of the couple who was with us started to "channel" one of the spirits. Channeling is where you allow the spirit to enter your body and they can use it to communicate with the living. She said that she was a female patient and wanted to talk with us. Then she started to talk in broken speech and had her voice go a few octaves higher. I decided to play along, so I asked this female patient some questions. What you are about to read is the word for word transcript of our conversation. The name of the woman (real one) is Sharon.

Bryan: What is your name?
Sharon (speaking like a little girl): Susan.
Bryan: How old are you?
Sharon: 12
Bryan: Why are you here?

Sharon: All alone.
Bryan: Do you have your parents?
Sharon: No, gone now.
Bryan: Did they leave you here, or did they pass?
Sharon: Don't know. Just gone I guess.

At this time, my friend leaned over to me and asked "What the hell are you doing? You don't believe her do you?". I said to him, "No, but I am just going to play along and see where she goes with it". I then continued my questioning.

Bryan: Do you have any family here?
Sharon: No. All alone.
Bryan: Do you have any friends here?
Sharon: I try, but they no play with me.
Bryan: What do you mean by no play?
Sharon: I try to be nice. I say hello, but they just keep walking. They say hello, but they no hear me. Makes me cry.
Bryan: How does the staff treat you?
Sharon: Doctor is bad man. He is very mean.
Bryan: Does he harm you?
Sharon: Yes! Yells a lot.
Bryan: Does he put his hands on you at all?
Sharon: No just yells. It's so cold. Why so cold?
Bryan: It's only 40 degrees outside. It's going to be cold.
Sharon: Why?
Bryan: It just is. Can you tell me which room is yours?
Sharon: Doctor is coming. Must go to bed.
Bryan: What does he look like?
Sharon: Must go to bed now. Doctor is yelling!
Bryan: Please tell us which one is your room.
Sharon (After a moment of silence): She has gone.

I thanked Sharon for doing this for us and told her to take her time to recover. Even though I didn't believe in any of what happened, it did give us something to check the records about. The experience did make me think though. What if on the off chance, it was real? Are the "friends" that Susan tries to contact us? The way that she described it, it sure does sound that way. It would explain as to why we do not answer them (spirits) when they try to talk to us. Same can be said the other way around. This was a theory that I would look into further. If not on this case, then on a future one.

We all sat in the group talking and soaking up what we just witnessed. After about fifteen minutes, we saw another group coming up a set of stairs at the end of the hallway. As they past, their flashlights shined on the staircase. What we saw next, shocked us all. The entire group (my friend and I included), saw a full bodied apparition. That's right, the "holy grail" of investigation.

My mind was racing a mile a minute. We all asked each other if we saw what we saw. I then asked my friend if he caught this thing on video. His response was a simple "Hell Yeah". Let me give you the best explanation of what we saw. To all of us it looked like a young woman with long hair. She looked like she was naked (as I would hope) or she had on very little clothing. It also looked as if she was sitting on her left hip with her lags wrapped behind her. This was an amazing site.

As I sat there collecting myself, something in my brain started to ask questions. Was it real? Why did we all see it at the same time? I thought to myself, there had to be some type of an explanation. Well, I was going to find out. I got up from my chair and made my way down to where the apparition was spotted. I told my friend to keep the video camera on me at all times. Some of the others in the group told me not to go towards it, because I would scare it away. Well, as an investigator, I had to see for myself. Another member of the group, a guy named Mike, accompanied me down the hallway. When we got to the staircase, we found the cause of the apparition.

It turns out that there was some plastic sheeting that had been crumpled up by the stairs. If you shined your light at a certain angle behind the plastic, it does make it look like the figure of a woman. We were able to recreate it a few times. Sharon told us that the woman was real and that we scared it away. Well, she can think what she likes. There is a saying in the paranormal business, when in doubt throw it out. So that's what we did. To say that we were disappointed would be an understatement. However, for a few moments, we had some excitement.

We returned to the group and discussed a few things before separating again. At this time, my friend and I took a break and had something to drink in the café. After the break was over, it was off to investigate the basement. The first room we checked out was called the Christmas room. The room had a Christmas tree, some ornaments, and some fake presents. So, you can clearly tell why it was called the Christmas room. This was the room where the kids would play when the building was used as a halfway house. I decided to do some Electronic Voice Phenomena (EVP) work. This is where you take an audio recorder and try to capture the voices of the spirits. You do this by asking questions and then pausing for 8 to 10 seconds for whatever it is to respond. After reviewing the recordings from this room, we came up empty.

We left the Christmas room and made our way to the machine shop and boiler rooms. The only claim of activity here was a large door would close on its own while someone was in a storage room. While investigating, we did see the door close. It closed on two people who opened the storage room and walk it. My friend and I checked the door and found the cause. The cause has nothing to do with the paranormal. The door is heavy enough that if it is pushed open past the tension point of the hinges, the door will close quickly on its own. We tested this multiple times with the same result.

The time was now three in the morning and most of the other investigators had left. My friend and I decided to check out the recreation room now that there were less people. We stayed in the room for about 45 minutes shooting video and conducting an EVP session. When we replayed the video, it didn't reveal anything. The audio however, did give us something. During the EVP session, I had asked the question "Is there anyone wishing to talk with us? We won't be here long, so now is your chance". When we played the audio back, we heard the voice of an elderly man. The man said to us "We are behind you, please walk slowly". This was my first real EVP. This is what I came here for. It made the trip all worth it.

The time was now five in the morning and we knew we had a long trip back to Minnesota. We packed up our gear, thanked Lori for allowing us to investigate, got in the car, and headed for home. This was a trip that I would never forget. I got to see some really cool things, see some historical places, and met some cool, smoking hot, and just plain weird people. Plus, we got to experience and document some paranormal things. If you are ever in the New York area, check out Rolling Hills. It's a great place and it is full of history. This was a great way to start off BPIMN.

CHAPTER 9:
INTERVIEW GONE WRONG

I would like to take a break from investigation stories for a bit. I will get back to them in the next chapter. Right now, I would like to tell you about an interview that I had with a prospective client. All of the cases that BIPMN takes or passes on, are first met with an interview. You want to do one to get a feel for the client, the environment, and to see what you might be getting yourself into. What you are about to read is real. I have changed the names of the people to protect their identities.

In April of 2009, I was contacted to perform an investigation for a man that claimed he was being tormented by an evil entity. After exchanging a few calls, we decided to meet at a restaurant in Elk River, MN. The "client" reserved the party room so we could have some privacy. We shook hands, exchanged a few pleasantries, and got down to business. Like I said before, I changed their names, so we call them Bruce and Rachel.

The first words out of Bruce's mouth were "What I am about to tell you, will make you think I am nuts. I assure you that I am not". This should have been a tip off that I was in for a wild ride. However, I was there to see it to the end. Bruce said that the spirit in his home was demonic and wanted to kill him. It all started for him when he noticed that the temperature would rise from 75 to 90 without any reason. Then, just as it raised, it would fall to lower than 30 degrees for no reason. He said that he knew something was wrong.

When I asked him if he ever had the temperature gauge looked at, he said that he didn't need to. He knew it was an evil spirit. He said it with such conviction, that it took me off guard a bit. I asked him how he knew it was demonic and his response was highly unusual. His response was "Oh, you could tell". That answer did fly with me, so I had to follow it up with another question. I asked Bruce, "What makes you so sure?". His answer sent up the first red flag of the interview. Bruce said, "He told me he was. He talks to me in my sleep". To me, this sounds like a dream. I then asked him what the entity tells him to do in his sleep. He responded, "It tells me to hurt my neighbors". I then had to ask, "Do you ever follow through with your harmful thoughts?". Bruce said, "No. I knock myself out before my rage takes over". I knew right then and there, that I knew I wasn't dealing with a guy playing with a full deck.

I think he could tell that I didn't believe him, so he said that he had proof to show me he was telling me the truth. The first piece of evidence he had to show was a melted clock. He had mentioned the clock to me in an earlier phone conversation. He took the clock out of a bag and handed it to me. I looked at it and said, "yep, it's a melted clock". I asked him how it happened. He said that it melted in the kitchen while he was cooking and baking (red flag #2). He also told me that the clock was hanging on the wall above the stove (red flag #3). I started to see where this one was going.

After he explained the clock to me, he handed me a picture. He said that he took this picture while the clock was melting. In the picture you can see a melted clock on the wall. I asked him what he thought brought on the melting of the clock. He told me that he was sitting in the living room and was hearing some banging coming from the kitchen. He told me that he got out of his chair, walked into the kitchen, and yelled "Stop making bangs and show yourself". He said that is when the clock began to melt. As I was listening to this,

I thought just one word. RIGHT! I asked him if the clock melted quickly or slow. He said that it melted over a 1 ½ hour period.

I would like to describe to you what was in the picture. I need to do this because, if you remember, he was cooking and baking when the clock started to melt. In the picture, you could see a melted clock on the wall above the stove. However, there was something else in the picture that caught my eye. Above the clock, there was a vacuum air vent. This is a vent that allows very hot air and steam to exit the house while cooking. Here is the conclusion I have about the clock. I do believe that the clock melted for about 1 ½ hours, but I do not think it was anything paranormal. What I think the caused the clock to melt is the heat from the stove and oven being rushed passed the clock and out the vent. The temperature was hot enough to melt the plastic clock.

The next piece of proof he had to show me was that of another picture. He said that he was standing outside his house and asked the spirits present to make themselves known. After he took the picture, he said that he had hundreds of orbs appear (red flag #4). BPIMN, along with other groups, do not put much weight behind orbs. Between 95% to 98% of orbs are dust, bugs, or moisture particles in the air. These things in the air reflect the light from the flash back into the camera lens. I also noticed something else about the picture. There was a lot of snow on the ground. My conclusion was that the orbs were just snowflakes reflecting the light.

After I told him my honest opinion, he got a little defensive and changed his point. He looked at me and said with a small tremor in his voice, "Look at the bottom. Do you see the face". I said "yes". What did I see? I saw a snowman that some neighbor kids had build in his front yard. I was really starting to think that I was wasting my time, but I wanted to see where he was going to go next.

The last piece of proof that he had to show me belonged to his friend Rachel. It was a simple white t-shirt with some scratches on the back of it. On the scratches was some dried blood. I thought to myself, "Ok, the blood is real. How could this have happened". After I asked her she responded that she was having a bad dream and woke up with the scratches. Her telling me of a bad dream raised red flag #5. I have cut myself on the nightstand while having a bad dream once.

I asked her if she had any pets that could have caused the scratches. She said no and leaned in close to me. She looked me in the eye and said "there is no explanation for what happened to me". I was taken aback by this and had to ask what her reasoning was. She told me that it was the spirit of her ex-husband coming back to get her. I asked why she thought it was her ex-husband. She said the he always hated her and that he would comeback to kill her. This interview has gone past the point of weird now.

My curiosity was getting the best of me, so I asked her what happened when she woke up. Rachel informed me that she couldn't move. She said that she could feel her ex-husband holding her down and trapping her on the bed. To me this sounds like a physical condition called sleep paralysis. It's a condition that happens to about 75% of the living pubic. It is just more pronounced in some than others. It has even happened to me twice.

This is what sleep paralysis is in a nutshell. When you sleep, your brain releases a chemical that keeps your arms and legs from moving. If it didn't, you would be physically acting out everything you were dreaming. You could end up breaking things, limbs, hurting yourself or someone else. Normally, when you wake up, you do it slowly. Then the chemical has time to wear off and you don't notice the paralysis. However, when you get waken suddenly, the chemical hasn't had time to wear off. Sleep paralysis can last for about twenty to thirty seconds and can scare the hell out of you if you've never had it before.

I told her what I felt about her situation was and she was quick to cut me off. Her response to me was that she has seen a doctor and he didn't believe in sleep paralysis. Well, I know that to be not true. I informed her that it's very common and that it happened to me, she just didn't want to hear it. After an evil stare from her, I asked her where she thought the scratches cam from. She said that her ex-husband put them there. She said that after she escaped her ex-husbands "death grip", she quickly sat up against the headboard. After she sat up, that's when she felt the scratches. Again, I started to think to myself. I asked her to describe her headboard to me. She said that it was an old wood one that was in need of repair. She said that she has it semi pieced together with some nails.

I asked her if it was possible that she was scratched by the nails. She said that there was no other explanation than her ex-husband harming her. She was convinced that the nails had nothing to do with it. These people weren't looking for an unbiased and scientific investigation. They wanted me to believe them 100%. I knew that if I took this case, I would be in real trouble.

I was then informed of the last major event that took place. Again, Rachel said that she was attacked by her ex. It happened after I had the initial phone call with Bruce. I couldn't wait to hear what this one was like. She said that she was walking to her bathroom when she felt the presence of her ex-husband spirit behind her. She said that after she was done using the bathroom, her ex-husband spirit pushed her out of the doorway. I asked her if she felt a hand on the back or a full on push. Rachel said it was more like a trip. Kind of like having the rug pulled out from under her.

I asked her for a description of the bathroom doorway. She said that it was a typical bathroom doorway with a two inch lip at the threshold. Meaning, that there was a small step down when exiting the bathroom. My next question to her was the time of day that this happened. She responded that it happened around two in the morning. I needed to know if she was fully awake or half asleep. She said that she was sleeping, but woke up after she heard her ex-husband say "I'll kill you". So to me that meant that she was half asleep and walking. This raised red flag #6 to me. I knew the question was a waste of time, but I asked if she could have just lost her balance since she wasn't fully awake. She just looked at me and said that it was her ex-husband trying to kill her.

After finishing the interview, I thanked the couple for their time. I informed them that I would take all the information that I gathered to my team and we'd talk it over. We shook hand, said our goodbyes, and I told them I would get back to them in a few days. I already knew that I wasn't going to waste my time with this case, but I kept my promise and talked to my team. As I explained what happened during the interview, my team started laughing. A friend of mine, Chad, said that a Hollywood writer couldn't come up with the kind of stuff I heard. In the end, we all agreed that we would not be taking this case.

Before I contacted Bruce about our decision, I contacted another group who had spoken with Bruce. It was a group located in northern Minnesota and lead by Adam Nori. I asked him about his thought of Bruce and Rachel. Adam asked me, "Is that the guy with the melted clock". I said yes. His advice to me was to get into my car and drive as far away as I could. That was all I needed to hear.

I called Bruce back about two days later. I was open and honest with him. I informed him that it was in my company's best interest to not go forward with an investigation. When asked why, I told him that it was not possible to give fair and honest answers to someone who doesn't want to listen to logical explanations. I told him that every piece of "evidence" he showed me, had a logical explanation. Bruce told me that I didn't know what I was doing and hung up the phone. This should be a lesson to anyone wanting to get into this field. Sometimes it's better to let some cases go.

CHAPTER 10: WEIRD CHICAGO

After returning from the east coast, I was bombarded with questions from people. People wanted to know what we saw, what did we hear, and what did you catch? I answered all the questions the best I could, but I had one question in the back of my mind. When was the next adventure going to happen? After seeing that face on video and catching those two EVP's, I wanted to set something up. Now the next question was, where do I go? I wasn't ready to go out on my own and BPIMN wasn't a full company yet. I knew I needed to get some more experience. So, I picked a place a little bit closer to home, Chicago. Being a Twins fan, I'm not that fond of Chicago (yes it's the White Sox fault). But, I could put that aside, and have some fun.

I was searching the web and found a website for a ghost tour called Weird Chicago. It is a company that is owned by world renowned paranormal researcher, investigator, and author Troy Taylor. The tours were on Thursday, Friday, and Saturday. I took them all. The Thursday and Saturday tours were investigation tours and the Friday tour was just an information tour. It was about one of Chicago's most famous ghost. I will cover that tour in a different chapter.

The Thursday tour started at 9pm. The bus for the tour would pick us up in the parking lot of the Hard Rock Café. The guide on our tour was a man named Adam Selzer. Adam is a children and ghost book author, musician, paranormal investigator, and general smart aleck. He is a great guy and I recommend his books (free plug). The Thursday tour was cool because it was just four of us, so Adam let us stay out at certain places longer than normal. In this chapter, I am only going to talk about a select few of them.

The first place that I want to talk about is a tattoo shop called Old Town Tatu. This place has had some form of activity for years. It was a funeral home before it was a tattoo shop. One of the former owners of the shop was a guy who went by the name Tapeworm. He used to live in an upstairs apartment. Tapeworm would hear bangs and thumps at night that would keep him up. He would also feel something that wasn't there hitting him. Also, some of his tattoo equipment would fault. According to witness reports, Tapeworm would also verbally confront spirits when they would cause problems. One night he got so fed up with all that was going on that he shouted at the top of his lungs "If I die, I'm coming back to kick all of your asses". He was of course talking about the spirits.

Well, as fate would have it, Tapeworm died of a heart attack one week after making that statement. The place stood quiet (activity wise) for a little while. The staff thought that maybe Tapeworm did beat up the spirits. However, the activity soon started up again. Especially when it came to the station that Tapeworm used to do his tattoos. If a new employee would work at his station, the equipment would fault or not work at all. However, if someone who Tapeworm knew and trusted worked there, the equipment would work just fine.

The only weird thing that happened here was in the basement. One of the girls on the tour was taking a picture of her boyfriend in the hallway. I was standing behind her and could see her boyfriend in the viewer of her digital camera. When she took the picture, something odd happened. In the photo, you could see the hallway and the wall at the end of it. Her boyfriend was nowhere in the photo. This one was a little difficult to explain. I am not a camera expert, but it could be a camera malfunction. If not, how do you explain her boyfriend not being there? That was the only thing. There was no video, audio, or interaction with Tapeworm felt by any of us.

The next stop on the tour was a place called The Glass Bending Factory. This is a place where back in the 1800's, H.H. Holmes would take some of his victims to be murdered. H.H. Holmes was the first serial killer in the United States. We were not allowed inside the building, but were told about some strange things that happen outside. One of the claims of activity, is if you say the name H.H. Holmes out loud, a light on a neighboring building would go on and off. I know that this sound weird, but all of us saw it happen. Was it H.H. Holmes making his presence known? Was it just a faulty light bulb that flickers every so often? Adam and I tend to agree on the later of the two.

Another claim of activity was hearing the sounds of crying coming from a fence behind the Glass Factory. Some "psychics" claim that it is crying of the victims. While we were there, we did not hear any crying. When I asked Adam what he thought it could be, he said that he believes it to be a bird cawing. After thinking about it, that explanation makes sense.

Our next stop was a bar called The Liars Club. This is a two story hard rock bar. Many famous bands such as Metallica, Twisted Sister, and Disturbed have all used the Liars Club for after show parties. There have been many fights and a few murders at the bar. We were told by the bar tender that just one week before we arrived, there was an attempted murder on the second floor bar. What happened? I am so glad you asked.

Apparently, some idiot got himself full of liquid courage and got lippy with a biker. This biker happened to belong to one of the most notorious biker gangs out there. I'm not going to name due to not wanting to die myself, but I think you can figure it out. After exchanging words, the idiot decided to get physical with the biker. At the start, there was just pushing by the idiot and laughing by the biker. Then, the idiot made the ultimate mistake. He spit on the biker. Well, the biker then beat this guy to a pulp and stabbed the guy multiple times. Fortunately for the idiot, the blade missed his major organs and arteries. The moron did survive and decided not to press charges. Sounds like a fun place to be right?

The claims of activity here were objects moving on their own, hearing strange voices, and seeing a full body apparition in the upstairs bar restroom. After hearing everything, we headed up to the second floor bar to start the investigation. When I got up there, I fell in love with it. The second floor bar was covered with KISS memorabilia. I'm a KISS nut and wanted to take the stuff home with me. I didn't just to let you know.

Since it was a small group, we spent about 40 minutes here. Adam and I were doing some EVP work asking questions and asking for signs of a presence. While we were in there, we didn't see or hear anything. However, when I played the audio back later, I did catch two strange EVP's. The first one happened as we were wrapping up the investigation. You hear me say "If there is anyone who wants to say anything, do so now. We are leaving soon". After that you can hear a whisper say "No, please wait". Could that have been someone from outside? Maybe, but we would have heard the voice with our own ears.

The second EVP is more creepy than anything I have ever caught. Even though we were done with the investigation, I kept the audio recorder going. I was the last one of the group to leave the bar, when I turn to say a final goodbye. The response I got almost sounded what many would say as "demonic". The only way I can describe it is like playing something back at a very low speed and then distorting it. It was just plain weird.

The last spot on the tour was the famous Congress Hotel. This is a very massive luxury hotel with very decorative ballrooms. Former US President Teddy Roosevelt gave many speeches here. The main claims of activity here came from the two main ballrooms. In the Grand ballroom, there claims are of seeing shadow people and hearing the playing of music. We spent 25 minutes in the room without any results. Some people in the group, Adam included, did get a little freaked out when a security guard appeared out of nowhere. We all got a good laugh from that.

We moved to the second ballroom. This one was located on the 3rd floor. This one was a large empty room with wood floors and a piano in the corner. The claims of activity in here are seeing dancing apparitions, hearing disembodies voices, and the feeling of being pushed out of doors. While in the room, we did not see or hear anything. I did get some very strange Electro Magnetic Field (EMF) readings. Everything on the planet gives off an EMF reading. A base reading for a room is between a 0.1 and a 1.2. There are some things such as microwaves and refrigerators that will give off higher readings. This is due to the electric wiring inside them. Sometimes if the appliances aren't grounded properly, the EMF readings can go off the charts (45 and 60).

The theory is that spirits, in order to manifest themselves, need to draw energy from the environment. When they do this, it causes a spike in EMF. Meaning that there is more energy present in one area. Now, we do not use EMF Detectors to find ghosts. Most of the time, people feel creeped out in places, have skin irritations, and feel like they are being watched. The EMF Detector can help find some of the appliances that give off high EMF readings. Some people are just over sensitive to these fields, and get some of the feelings that I mentioned above.

The ballroom itself was a 0.2, but the piano in the room was another story. The piano was an old style, wooden one from the 1920's. There were no electrics in it at all, I checked. The piano was giving off a reading of 5.3, very unusual for something with no electrics. What was even more unusual, was the bench. Right where someone would be sitting, I got a reading of 8.2. The readings were concentrated to the piano only. The farther away from the piano I got, the lower the readings would go. I looked through the walls and found some exposed wiring. However, the wiring only gave off a 1.8 reading. So, I was able to rule that out. I searched above the piano and underneath it. The readings would be low.

This is something that I m going to label paranormal. I do not have an explanation for it at this time. Was it possible that a spirit was still at the piano? If so, who could it be? Did it think that we were a group coming to hear him/her play? These are questions that I ask myself a lot. I would like to go back and do a full investigation with BPIMN. I enjoyed going on the tour. I enjoyed my time on the tour and have recommended it to everyone that I talk to. Adam isn't with the tour anymore, but Troy Taylor will hook you up with a good time. If you are interested, check out their website at www.weirdchicago. com for more information. Hey there's another free plug.

CHAPTER 11:
HAUNTED HISTORY PART 1

I am now going to tell you about two of the more famous ghosts in the Chicago area. One of them you have heard about, the other might be a bit more obscure. These were stories we were told on the second day of the tour. We never got off the bus for this one, but we did visit the locations. The first one I'm going to talk about is the most famous. Who am I talking about? None other than Resurrection Mary.

No one can pinpoint who Mary is, but it has been narrowed down to two people. Most of the reports and descriptions lead to a girl named Mary Brigovy. The other is a girl named Anna "Mary" Norkus. Both girls died in automobile accidents, Brigovy in 1934 and Norkus in 1927. This is how the story goes. It is told the same way for both girls. Mary was dancing at the Oh Henry (now known as the Willowbrook) ballroom. At one point during the evening, she got into an argument with her boyfriend and stormed out of the ballroom. According to some reports, the last words she said (to her boyfriend) were, "I'd rather face the cold rain then spend another minute with you". Wow! What a... oh sorry.

After she left the ballroom, she started walking down Archer Road. She didn't get very far, when she was struck by a hit and run driver. She had died a few minutes later. Her parents (not sure which girl), had her buried in Resurrection Cemetery in her favorite white dress. After the burial was over, that's when the sightings started to happen. Why? I am not sure, but I do have a theory. Remember, the hit and run driver was never caught. It is possible that she was waiting until the identity of her "killer" is known.

The most well documented sighting happened in 1939. It happened to a man named Jerry Palus. He described everything that happened to him in a 1982 interview. According to Mr. Palus, he was at the Oh Henry ballroom with some friends looking for girls (a man after my own heart). He was standing by the bar listening to the band, when he saw a young, beautiful, blonde woman standing by herself. He went over to her and asked her to dance. The two of them danced the entire night and even kissed a bit. He did notice that while dancing, her hands were cold as ice. Keep that in mind for later.

Once the night was over, Jerry asked her what her name was. She told him Mary. Jerry then asked Mary if she wanted a ride home. She agreed to except the ride. Jerry asked her where she lived, and she responded that she lived on Daemon Road. As they started driving, she begged him to take her down Archer Road. That just happens to be the road that Resurrection Cemetery is on. Jerry was confused as to why, but he was smitten with this girl, so he went along with it. As they were driving past the cemetery, Mary yelled for Jerry to stop the car. He did and Mary got out of the car. Jerry got out of the car to ask what was going on. Mary grabbed his hand and told him to wait by the car. She then turned around and walked towards the cemetery front gates. Jerry watched her walk away and then vanished before his eyes. He dismissed it as him being too tired.

The next day, Jerry went down to Daemon Road where Mary said she lived. As he approached the front door of the house, the door opened. An old woman met Jerry at the door. He introduced himself and told the woman that he was looking for a young woman named Mary who lived there. The lady said that no one by that name lived there. As the lady turn to close the door, Jerry noticed a picture on a table. Jerry pointed at the photo and said "That's her. That's the girl that I was dancing with last night". The woman turned pale and said that he couldn't have been dancing with her. She then informed Jerry that the girl in the photo was her daughter and that she's been dead for five years. All of a sudden, Jerry had an explanation as to why Mary's hands were ice cold. He used to work in a mortuary and it felt like the hands of a corpse. Jerry knew that he had danced with a ghost.

Over the years, the sightings of Mary were sporadic and didn't keep to any time frame. People driving down Archer Road would see a woman in a glowing white dress walking on the side of the road. A few taxi drivers who had gotten lost on Archer Road, say they have asked a young lady for directions back into Chicago. In return for her help, they would give her a ride to anywhere she wanted free of charge. The taxi drivers would be speechless as they would see the girl disappear in their back seat.

There is a story that Mary had left physical proof of her existence. One night in 1976, a couple was out for a drive down Archer Road. As the drove past the cemetery, they claimed to see a woman inside the gates holding onto the bars. The couple doubled back to see if the girls was in trouble, only to find that there was no one there. The next day, the couple went back to the same spot where they had seen the woman. To their amazement, the bars on the gate looked warped. To them, it looked like someone was holding the bars and melted the pattern of their fingers into them. The couple immediately informed the local authorities.

After inspecting the bars, some "experts" in the paranormal field said that the marks did look like fingers. They said that the segments of the finger joints could clearly be seen. Over the years, people would come to the site, take pictures, and hope to see Mary. However, the cemetery officials say that the "damage" was caused by a truck that had backed into the bars. They also said that there is no evidence, that a spirit or any other type of paranormal phenomena caused the damage. Eventually, the cemetery got fed up with people coming just to see the bars, that they had them removed in the 1990s. To this day, there are still reports of feeling uneasy when by the spot of the bars.

So, is Mary still roaming the grounds of the cemetery? There hasn't been a reported sighting of her for over twenty years. It is surly possible that she is waiting for her killer to either confess to the hit and run or to pass on himself/herself. We still keep look outs for her, hoping that one day, she will grace us with her presence once again.

The other famous ghost or should I say story, is that of the Grimes Sisters. Why do I say story? Well there haven't been many sightings of them, but the story lives on to this day. Barbara (15) and Patricia (13) Grimes, were two young girls who went missing on December 28th, 1956. Their bodies were found naked, under snow, in a ditch five days later. Like Mary, their killer has never been found.

The sisters were huge fans of Elvis Presley and were going to the theater to see his movie *Love Me Tender* for the 11th time. It is a fact that they made it to the theater because they were spotted in the popcorn line around 9:30pm. They were also spotted on an Archer Road bus around 11pm that same evening. That was the last time anyone seen the girls alive. Or was it?

After that night, the girls were seen in multiple locations. Just a mere 24 hours after they disappeared, someone spotted the two girls who fit their description at a restaurant called Angelo's. The same day, they were spotted by a train conductor at the Great Lakes Naval Training Center in the Chicago suburb of Glenview. A few days later, they were supposedly seen in Englewood, IL. According to George Pope, a clerk at the Unity Hotel (it's not there anymore), denied two girls a room because of their ages. The description he gave of the two girls, matched that of the Grimes sisters. The most unusual sighting was on the day their bodies were found. According to three employees of a record store called Kresege, the girls were spotted listening to Elvis records. This last one was very weird.

Getting back to the girls death. They were found in a ditch on German Road. A driver in a truck, saw what he thought were mannequins on the side of the road. When he got out to put them in the back of his truck to take them to town, he noticed that they were too lifelike. To his horror, he realized that they were real girls and went to get the sheriff. It was determined, after the coroner did his inspection, that the girls were alive when they were dumped in the ditch. The cause of death was ruled death by freezing.

This brings up many questions. Why were they naked? You would think they knew or trusted whomever did this to them. Meaning, they felt comfortable before all hell broke loose. Another question is, why didn't they get off at their normal bus stop? That leads to another question, where did they get off? Who were they with? Unfortunately, we will never know the answers to these questions. This goes down as an unfortunate accident.

So, why do these spirits hang around? Are they just waiting for the deaths of whomever did these acts to them? You would think that would be enough. I think that death is not the justice that they want. They want someone to be legally charged, tried, and sentenced. I believe that the spirits will then find peace. If you ever are in the Chicago area, take the Resurrection Mary tour. It is a lot of fun and very educational.

CHAPTER 12:
WRESTLING AND MCGH

When I returned from Chicago, I knew it was back to reality. It was back to work at my security job and also back into the wrestling ring. I also, started a mini wrestling camp. I wanted to teach a group of "want to be's" the way pro wrestling was to be done. Plus, it was some extra cash coming in. The wrestling business was picking up again, so I put the paranormal pursuits on hold for a short bit.

In January of 2009, I got to team up with a wrestler whom I grew up watching on television. My regular tag partner, The Spiderbaby, got to do a six man tag team match with the one and only Tito Santana. Tito is a former two time WWF Intercontinental and two time WWF Tag Team Champion. He is also a 2004 WWE Hall of Fame Inductee. I felt like I was a little kid. Even though most of us on the card had over ten years of experience in the business, but we extracted as much knowledge from him as we could. At the after party, he was telling us road stories about the business and the fun they had on the road. About 90% of the stories he told, I can't repeat. I couldn't do them justice. Besides, they are way too dirty for this book. Take my word, they were funny as hell.

Over the next few months, I spent most of the time wrestling. I won tag team titles with Spiderbaby and made some good money. In August of 2009, I went back into the paranormal field. I took a weekend off of work and wrestling to do a case in southern Illinois. I got the gig through a hook up with Troy Taylor. The group is called the Macoupin County Ghost Hunters (MCGH). The company is run by Dan and Kelly Davis and their lead investigator Loren Hamilton. This was a great chance to investigate with and learn from a separate company. The case we had in store was an old Opry House in Winchester, Illinois.

The Opry was an old airplane hanger that was converted into a country music bar back in the 1960's. This place is literally in the middle of nowhere. So, if something would have happened to us that required medical attention, we would have been screwed. I drove past the place numerous times before I found it. When I arrived, I met the rest of the people who were there. We were given an introduction and brief history of the place. We were then given a tour of the hot spots of activity. Then it was time for a small break and then we were split into groups. One of the guys in my group was Mark Eckhoff. Mark helped me sent up some equipment and asked me about how I investigate. He's a really nice guy and is now a senior investigator and the Iowa Representative for BPIMN.

I set up a static night vision camera in the dance hall of the Opry House. I pointed it towards the stage because people have claimed to see full bodied apparitions there. I also set up a digital audio recorder. I was told that my group would be starting on the outside grounds. I then quickly set up a hand held night vision camera and met my group outside. Kelly Davis was the leader of our group.

Our first mission was to contact the spirit of a Native American. It was said that this spirit roamed the grounds of the Opry. I had my video camera ready to catch anything the "might" happen and Mark had his K2 Meter ready. The K2 Meter is another type of Electromagnetic Field (EMF) meter. Instead of giving a digital number reading, it gives the level of EMF using a range of colored lights. The lights range from green (lowest) to red (highest). Since spirits are energy, the theory is that they can communicate through the K2 with yes and no answers. Meaning, lighting the lights once for yes and twice for no. I have seen this done on television many times before, so I was hoping to see it in person. Others in the group had still photo cameras and Kelly had dowsing rods.

This was the first time that I had seen dowsing rods in action. Dowsing has been around for centuries. They are mainly used to find underground water supplies. They are L shaped wired that are held in the hands. The rods will then move "on their own" when someone is close to underground water or a high EMF field. Kelly's rods (that sounds perverted) were a tad bit different. She had the L shaped rods, but hers had crystals at the ends of them. When I asked why, she stated that it helps the spirit energy manifest. You should have seen my face when she said that.

First, Kelly asked for the spirit to make its presence known. She asked for the spirit to give her a yes answer. The rods then crossed in an X pattern. The she asked for the spirit to release the rods and they went back to parallel. Kelly then asked the spirit to show her no and the rods split in opposite directions. Again, she asked the spirits to release the rods and they went back to parallel. Was this real? Was this a spirit making these rods move or was I seeing something else? I had some questions going through my mind and I wanted to find out the answers.

Kelly then asked the spirit if it was a male and the rods crossed yes. After its release, she asked for the spirits name. The rods then crossed in a no direction. The rods stayed in this position for a few minutes. At that time, a few coyotes howled in the background. Kelly then asked the spirit if that was his brothers communicating. The rods then crossed yes. I thought that it was too good to be true. I decided to zoom in on Kelly's hands the next time the rods would cross. When she asked the spirit if he was angry and the rods crossed yes. I zoomed in to see if possibly Kelly was moving the rods. Unfortunately, I could not see clearly. Makes me think though.

After losing contact with the spirit, we moved to another location on the grounds to try again. One of the others in the group stated that they saw a dark figure walking in the woods next to us. I turned to look, but saw nothing. Kelly used the rods again and determined that it was the same spirit as before. This was a very warm night, around 75 to 80 degrees. Why am I saying this? When we were doing an EVP/K2 session, my left arm started to get really cold. There was no breeze or anything. The coldness was concentrated on a one spot of my left forearm. On that spot, I have a tattoo of a member of the rock band KISS in full makeup. Why is that something you should know? I'm glad you asked.

I knew from reading the history of a few Native American cultures, that some of the warriors would paint their faces before going into battle. Was this a spirit trying to make contact with me? I was going to try and find out. I took it upon myself to ask the "spirit" a question. I asked it if he was making my arm cold. The rods crossed in an X pattern meaning yes. We then did a temperature scan to record the coldness. My core body temp was at 98 degrees and my right arm was at 96 degrees. However, my left forearm was at 85 degrees. That is an 11 degree difference. Kelly then asked the spirit if he liked my tattoo. The rods crossed yes. The she asked the spirit if my tattoo reminded him of himself. The rods then crossed yes again. The rods then fell silent and we lost all contact with this spirit.

I do not know what to think of this nor do I know how to explain it. Why was it fascinated with my tattoo? Was the coldness I felt on my arm a spirit grabbing me? Why would the spirit only communicate through the dowsing rods and not the K-2? I am still skeptical a bit on the whole dowsing rod thing too. While it is possible that a spirit was communicating, it also could have been the subconsence. What do I mean by this? Your mind can make your muscles move involuntary and you then can move things without knowing it. Most of the time, these muscle movements are so small that you can't see them. Was it this that caused the rods to move? I don't know, but there has to be an explanation. I just don't have one yet.

After we completed the outside rounds, our group went inside to investigate the main dance hall. I walked around and did some basic filming and EVP work. There was nothing caught on video that I couldn't explain away. Likewise, with the audio. There were way too many people in this one place. MCGH had 25 people investigating at one time which caused contamination and all EVP's had to be thrown out. This was exactly the same when we did the area behind the stage. We were doing audio recordings to contact a spirit of a girl. The only voices we heard came from a group that was outside. That is the problem you encounter when there are too many people.

We took a break from investigating for about an hour. When the break was over, we made the trip into the woods. We were told there was an old cemetery in the middle of it. I was intrigued since I love old cemeteries. To get to the cemetery, it was an uphill climb. The climb was only about a half mile, but to a big guy like me, it felt like 10 miles. When I reached the top, I thought my legs were going to fall off. Even though most of us were tired from the climb, I did make a small joke about it. I said that the trip back down would be a lot faster. If you trip, just tuck your head and roll. We all got a good laugh.

The cemetery was something to see. There were gravestones scattered all over the area. Most of the stones had death dates ranging from 1850 – 1920. There were a small number of stones that dated before the 1800's. I took video of them because I like them. Morbid I know. As a group, we did an EVP session to see if there was anything with us. I only recorded about 35 minutes of it since my camera battery was about to die. Rose, MCGH company psychic, grabbed the dowsing rods and tried to make contact. When she asked the spirits to show her a yes answer, the rods went in opposite directions. When she asked for a no answer, the rods crossed. This was completely opposite of what Kelly was doing earlier.

As I watched her doing everything opposite, I had a question running through my head. Which way is the right way? They can't both be correct. I am not one who believes in psychic ability, so I would just let it play out and see what happens. As the investigation was going on, a few people in the group heard what they called footsteps. Did I believe them? Yes I did. Was it something paranormal? I would have to say no. We were in the middle of the woods. It was more than likely to be a deer or a coyote. Some of the others were convinced that it was paranormal. I think these were people who were desperate to see something. Unfortunately, there are far too many of them.

We stayed in the woods for about an hour. The only strange thing that happened was out of nowhere all these dogs showed up. There were about six in total. There was this small cute beagle that I wanted to take home with me. However, I did not. They were very well mannered dogs that showed up and sat down next to us. Was it paranormal? No, but it was weird.

We then headed back into the Opry House. We sat around and talked as a group about what we had experienced. Kelly did mention the thing about my arm even though I'm not sure that it was paranormal. A few other people said that they saw a man walking up the driveway. They said that he walked about 30 feet and then vanished. Only their word to go by, no one caught it on video. As I was wrapping up my equipment, my foot caught a cable that forced one of my cameras to fall on the floor. There was this old woman there who then said to me "The spirits here don't like your fancy gadgets". I asked her what she meant. She said that because I was trying to find explanations for the claims, that the spirits caused my camera to fall. I told her that I tripped the cord, but she didn't want to hear it. He was convinced that a spirit did it. I just laughed it off. Remember what I said about people wanting things to be true?

So, what is my overall impression of the Opry House? Well I don't do impressions, but I will tell you what I think. I do not believe that the Opry is haunted. I have no solid proof, nor any real personal experiences. I am not counting the arm thing. It was a great experience and I did have a good time. I met some great people and some kooky people. If by the off chance that the place is haunted, the spirits didn't want to play that night.

CHAPTER 13: 1ST LOCAL CASE

In September of 2009, BPIMN was given its first local case. When I say local, I mean in Minnesota. The place we were investigating was a hotel located in Sauk Centere, MN. Sauk Centere is located off of Interstate 94 about thirty minutes north of St. Cloud, MN. The hotel will remain nameless due to privacy reasons. I read about this hotel in many books and saw a few video clips online. I then contacted the owner and set up the date of September 19th, 2009 as the date of the investigation.

I made the phone calls to the team and we headed out. The team was a foursome consisting of BPIMN'S second in command Sarah Frigon, two investigators in training Erin Roed and Tom Smith, and myself. When we arrived, we met in the dining area and had dinner. During the dinner, we were met by the owner Kelley. We talked for a bit, finished dinner, and then brought in our equipment. After setting up a command center in the conference room, it was time for the tour. Kelley brought in a guest to give us the tour. Former member of a local paranormal radio show Adrian Lee. We were given the history of the hotel and shown where all the claimed "hot spots" for activity were located. When the tour was over, we thanked Kelley and Adrian for their time and began setting up the equipment.

I had Tom set up a static night vision camera in the lobby. I had him aim the camera at the French doors that lead to the bar area. There were claims of seeing a full body apparition in these doors.

We covered the rest of the hotel with digital audio recorders and hand held video cameras. We then split into two groups (Erin & Sarah and Tom & I), and started the investigation on the hotels third floor.

Tom and I started in the 3rd floor laundry room. In this room, Kelley (the owner) claimed to have been choked by a spirit named Raymond. Raymond, in life, was the town "pimp" and loved to manhandle women. We started by doing an EVP session. Tom and I introduced ourselves and asked if Raymond was present in the room. The room stayed very quiet during the entire hour we were in there. After the all was said and done in this room, we had no personal experiences and no evidence on video or audio.

While we were in that room, Sarah and Erin were in Room 17. This was known as Lucy's room. Lucy was the main prostitute in town back in the 1900's. Lucy was murdered, sort of speak, by her pimp Raymond. Now, he didn't actually kill her, but he tormented her enough that she committed suicide. The claims of activity in this room are seeing Lucy sitting on the bed with a decaying face. If a man sits in one of her favorite chairs, she will push him out of them. The metal hangers in the bathroom will move and clang by them selves. Also, the door of the room would slam on its own.

The girls did EVP work and shot video. They had no personal experiences while in the room. I then decided that we should switch rooms. Erin and Sarah to the laundry room and Tom and I in Room 17. As Tom and I were entering Room 17, Sarah mentioned to me that she had a theory of how the door could slam. She told me that while in the room, she noticed that the floors are uneven. Meaning, that the door could swing shut on a down slope. Tom and I decided to test this theory. Before we did that, we wanted to see if we could get pushed out of the chairs. So, Tom and I sat in the two chairs. We sat in the chairs for about 30 minutes without any activity. Granted, we only tested it for a half hour, but it does give way to two possibilities. Either Lucy isn't there or Lucy likes big guys. Why are the girls who like big guys dead? I just can't win.

We next checked out another claim of activity the feeling of being watched and the feeling of "creepy skin". That is when you feel like someone is lightly touching you. Most of the time, this is caused by the people being EMF hypersensitive. Tom and I took our EMF detector and we found the cause of the creepy feeling. We found what we call in the paranormal field a fear cage. A fear cage is caused by being bombarded by high EMF from all sides. Well, this room had one.

As we were testing the television, we found that it gave off a reading of 3.4. On the other side of the room was a clock radio. The radio was giving off a reading of 9.6. That is very high. Of the reports of being watched, about 80% of them come from when you would be laying down on the bed. Not only do they deal with the fear cage, but the clock is right by their head. The 9.6 will really mess with someone's head if they are hypersensitive.

Now onto the mystery of the slamming door. We checked the floor and found that it was uneven just like Sarah said. When we inspected the door, we found that it was a very heavy wood door. When it opens, it's on an incline and closes on a decline. They only way for it to stay open, was to push it until it catches on the carpet. Now, if you push it hard onto the carpet, the door isn't going anywhere. However, if it just barely catches the carpet, it could come loose and close.

We tested this by the use of two methods. Tom pushed the door just barely onto the carpet so it would stay open. We then walked on the floor next to the door. Some of the floorboards were a little loose and if you stepped on them in the right spot, the door would come loose. Then the heavy door would slam shut on its own. We then tried to see if wind forces would cause it to slam. With the door barely catching, we got the same result. We found that if you sat on the bed or threw your bags on the bed with force, it would cause the door to come loose and slam shut. We feel that we have debunked the slamming of the door. Now keep this in mind, we were not present when other people experienced it. We are not saying that they are wrong, we just say it's an alternate explanation.

After spending the time debunking the claims on the third floor, we moved to the first floor. We were not able to investigate the second floor due to the only room with activity was occupied by another couple. We did ask them (in the morning) if they had any experiences. They said no. On the first floor we investigated the dining room. The claims of activity in here are the silverware moving on its own. This one was going to be difficult to do. The only thing that could be done was to set the silverware, take photos, and come back later to see if they moved. None of them did, but we did notice that the ends of all the forks were slightly magnetic. This could cause the silverware to move.

After a small break and changing tapes in the static camera, we headed down to the basement area. The claims of activity down here are seeing a little boy who is looking for his mother. An apparition of a woman named Christena, disembodied footsteps, voices, tugging of clothes and hair, and an evil, dark, shadowy mass. We were told that if we came across the evil mass that we should avoid it at all costs. Yeah! Like that would happen.

We all started an EVP session in the Snowman Room. It was named that because of the big snowman in it. Tom and Erin sat on the north side of the room (by the entrance) while Sarah and I sat on the south side (far wall). We started by contacting Christena and the boy. After about thirty minutes with no luck, we took a small break to readjust the cameras. Sarah took the hand held night vision camera and pointed it at Tom and Erin. At one point, I saw some movement on the floor by Tom. I asked Tom if he felt anything by his feet and he said "No, I'm just moving them". At that moment, Erin screamed and demanded all lights to be turned on. After a few minutes of calming her down, she said that she felt fingers brush her hair. To cover all bases, Tom and I searched the area above and around where Erin was sitting. We found no spider webs or falling plaster.

When I reviewed the tape at home, I checked for anything that looked out of the ordinary. Just before the hair brushing happened, the camera goes out of focus. After it comes back into focus, you can see a dark mass form behind Tom and Erin just before her hair is brushed. Was it real? Did something paranormal come in contact with Erin? Was it Christena or the boy? Can't say for sure. I only have her word to go on. The video leading up to it is cool to see.

After the inspection was over, it was time to go lights out again. Erin was not too happy with that. For the next half hour, nothing happened. Then, the four of us all hear a strange noise. To me it sounded like a popcorn machine making popcorn. The only thing, the hotel doesn't have a popcorn machine. Was it mice? If so, they would have to have been very big mice. Then, the sound started to get louder and closer to us. What could it be?

As we listened, Erin said that the noise sounded like horses walking on concrete. Sarah then mentioned to all of us that the basement used to be the old horse stables back in the early 1900's. Were these the sounds of horses from the past? It was an interesting thought. But, why would they be making contact? Tom and I decided to find out. As we walked out into the hallway, the footsteps started to walk away from us. As I walked down to where the footsteps were leading me, Tom stayed about 10 steps behind me. Sarah stayed in the snowman room with Erin to se if anything was trying to separate us.

The steps lead me into a room where the hotel keeps their soda syrup machines. There also storage rooms in the area. I followed the footstep sounds until I felt some loose rock below my feet. I turned my flashlight on for safety and that's when the footsteps stopped. It turns out that the steps lead me to an area where the hotel owners were doing some digging. Kelley and her husband had found some bones under a staircase and were digging for some more. The bones that were found turned out to be animal bones. After a few minutes, I turned my flashlight off to see if the footsteps would start up again. Unfortunately, they did not.

Were the ghosts of the horses trying to tell us where they were buried? This is an odd experience and I am going to label it paranormal. I am not going to say it was ghost related, but I don't have an explanation yet. While I was searching the area, I found one of the coolest pieces of evidence I have caught. When we were taking the tour of the hotel around nine in the evening, no one on the tour or any of the hotel staff were wearing high heels. Now, it was three in the morning, and in a back storage room I saw a woman's high heeled boot print coming out of a puddle of water. I am not sure how to explain this one. I have it both on video and on still photo. Again, it goes into the books of paranormal.

At 3:15 in the morning, we decided to go back to the first floor to investigate the bar area. The claims of activity in here are seeing full bodied apparitions, hearing glasses breaking, and hearing disembodied voices. We were in the bar for about 45 minutes and did not have any experiences. At four in the morning, we broke down our equipment and went to bed. We got up at ten in the morning and had breakfast in the hotel restaurant. Many of the other patrons, who knew why we were there, would come up to us and ask us what we saw. We just told them the truth and say "Not sure. Need to look at the footage". After breakfast, we loaded up the cars and headed for home.

All in all this was a great experience. We were able to explain most of the things away and had some great experiences in the basement. I would like to bring BPIMN back there in the future and concentrate solely on the basement. The hotel is a great place, the staff was great, and the food was great. If you are ever driving through Sauk Centere, ask to stay at the haunted hotel. Just ask any business, and they will tell you which one it is. Who knows, maybe you can share a room with a ghost.

CHAPTER 14: BACK WITH MCGH

On October 31st, 2009, I went back to southern Illinois to investigate with MCGH. The place we were going to investigate was the James Eldred House in Eldred, IL. This place happened to be just down the road from the Opry House (the place I investigated with MCGH before). The house was difficult to find. It was just off the main road through town, but it was very well hidden. I stopped at a local American Legion in town to ask for directions. After about twenty minutes of explaining to the "locals" what I was looking for, I was given directions. When I finally got there, I realized that I had driven past this place four times. MCGH should have put a ghost signal in the air or something.

Waiting at the front of the house was Kelly Davis and Loren Hamilton. We waited for about 45 minutes while other investigators arrived. Just like the Opry House, there were too many people at the site. But, I planned to make the most of the situation. Why? This was Halloween night and according to stories, a lot of activity happens on this night. I could only hope.

After everyone had arrived and heard the instructions, we were split up into groups. I was put in the group with Loren. Also in the group was this kid named Josh whom I met at the Opry House case. Also with us was his sister Beth. She was a very nice woman and very nice on the eyes as well. I was very happy to have her with. We also had this nimrod in the group. He was a friend of Josh, although

Josh tried to keep his distance. This kid thought that everything was caused by a ghost and wouldn't listen to any type of explanation. The worst part about this kid is that he would not shut up. I wanted to make him a ghost if you know what I mean.

Our first stop for the group was on the first floor. On the first floor was a small bedroom to the right of the front door. It was closed off to us due to the floor had caved in. I will cover the claim in this room a little later in the chapter. To the left of the front door is the guest parlor. There are no claims in this room. Down the hall is a family room and Mr. Eldred's den. The claims in here are hearing footsteps and small objects moving. All the way in the back of the first floor was the kitchen. Here the claims of footsteps and whispers. There was also the claim of seeing the apparition of one of the Eldred's daughters. Her name is believed to be Emma.

As we investigated the first floor, Josh told me that he was getting some weird spikes on his EMF meter. He said that his meter went from a 0.1 to a 3.5 while he was standing still. Then it meter went back down to a 0.1 reading. He then walked along the wall of the family room and was able to track the 3.5 for about ten feet and then it dissipated into a wall by the kitchen. Was it a spirit? Can't say for sure, but it is odd to get a high EMF spike in a place with no electricity. We are labeling this paranormal since we do not have any real explanation for it.

While I was investigating the first floor den, I caught a very good piece of video evidence. I was walking around filming the whole room and decided to focus my attention on the den's closet door. Josh, who was standing behind me, asked me a question. I turned to answer him while keeping my camera on the door. I did not see it live, but when I reviewed the tape, the den closet door moved on it's own a little bit. This may not seem like a big deal to most, but to an investigator it is. I have ruled out the wind since all the windows were shut and paint sealed. There was also no wind that night. It wasn't the floorboards, because if it was, it would have happened many times and to other investigators. This a cool piece of evidence.

Josh, Beth, myself, and a few others convened in the kitchen to try and make contact with Emma. As we sat there, a small pebble rolled into the kitchen. I went out into the hall to see if anyone was out there and to see if anyone had kicked or thrown a pebble. All of them said no. That loud mouth annoying idiot said that it was a ghost trying to make contact. I should have known he was going to say something like that. As I was walking back into the kitchen, I looked at the wall where the group had been standing by. I saw that a lot of plaster coming off the wall and falling on the floor. I do not believe it was anything paranormal. I think that someone out in the hall had kicked a small piece of plaster and it rolled into the kitchen.

We did not experience anything else while on the first floor. Well, not those of us with level headed minds. Josh's goofy friend kept saying that Emma was touching him and asking him questions. He just wouldn't shut up about it. I have all of his annoying psycobabble on tape. Be very glad you were not with on the investigation. You would want to find a place to hang yourself. If you were on this investigation, I need go no further about this guy. But, I will.

Our next stop was the second floor and the attic. This is where the Eldred's had their bedrooms and playroom/nursery. The master bedroom is right at the top of the staircase. The son's and daughter's rooms are down the hall. Nothing happened to us while we were in this area this time. That is a clue to something that happened to us later. Captain goof had another self proclaimed experience in the attic. He was yelling at the top of his lungs and making a scene.

He claimed to have seen a full bodied apparition looking at him and him alone. None of the other people who were up in the attic saw anything. When I asked him to describe what the apparition looked like, I could not believe what he told me. He said the apparition was a male, wearing black pants, black coat, and a black hat. Well, that's a cool description, but that also described about 60% of the men on this investigation. What a dork!

The next top for us was the basement. Down here is where the Eldred family made their own cheese. One of the rooms had a giant cheese wheel in it. The other rooms were semi blocked off. They had pallets, large wood beams and huge rocks that were holding up the collapsed floor of the 1st floor bedroom. The claims of activity in the basement were being pushed off the cheese wheel if you sat on it. There were also the reports of disembodied footsteps. This one is weird, because it is an all dirt floor. Well, no one other then the huge dork had any experiences here. Again, he said that he could feel himself being push and falling to the ground. There were many divots in the floor and rocks to trip over. He didn't want to hear any explanation. This guy wanted to see a ghost. He ended up tricking his mind into believing everything.

As I was leaving the cheese room, Beth had called me over to her in one of the blocked rooms. She claimed that one of the doors had moved on its own. So, I went over to have a look. At the door, but did check her out too. As I looked at the door and saw that it was a heavy wood and metal door. It would not move very well without some type of force. Again, there wasn't any wind flowing through the basement. We tried to recreate the movement by blowing on the door (silly I know) and by taping it. We were not able to recreate the door moving. This goes down as a personal experience for her. It was not caught on tape. Because she is hot, I have to believe her right?

The last area to be covered as a group was the grounds. Loren took us around and showed us where all the old foundations used to be and the outer stone wall. He also showed us the gravesite of a Native American that is buried on the grounds. The claims of activity on the grounds were seeing the spirit of the Native American walking the grounds. We didn't stay out here very long, but nothing happened while we were there.

After all the split groups had covered all the areas, we all gathered in the kitchen. The group was asked to talk about anything that they experienced or had caught on video/audio. One lady in the group said that every time that she looked in the first floor bedroom, she would get a massive headache. However, when she would walk away from the room, the headache would go away. Kelly was surprised to hear her say that and then went into a story about a traveling salesman. Apparently, the salesman had died in the house of a head wound. No one knows who the salesman was or how he got the head wound. The lady stated that she was "somewhat psychic" and was probably picking up on his energy. I only have her word to go off of. Do I believe her? Not really.

The loudmouth then had to tell everyone the stuff that he claimed to have seen. Even the people who weren't in our group didn't believe him. I was hoping beyond hope that someone would take him out back and shove him down the outhouse hole. He kept playing back his audio tapes, but nothing was on it. He then had the insane thought to tell us that since we didn't believe him, the spirits didn't want to be heard. MORON!!!!!

At this point, we all took a 10 minute break. Most people went outside and got warm by the bonfire. I went out there for a little bit too, but only because Beth was out there. Then, we were told that the last stop on the tour, was the town cemetery. This was the cemetery that the Eldred's were buried in. I did not go with, I decided to stay in the house and investigate with Beth and Josh. Thankfully, the annoying loud mouth went with the group to the cemetery. The three of us started our investigation in the second floor master bedroom. We had our video and audio recorders going and had the K-2 Meter ready to make contact with any of the Eldred family.

We did and EVP session by asking if any of the family would like to make their presence known. After sitting in silence for about twenty minutes, the three of us heard what sounded like footsteps coming down the hallway. We got us to search the floor, but could not see anyone. We searched each room before returning to the master bedroom. As we continued, Beth said that she thought she heard a ball bouncing up in the attic. Josh said that he heard it too, but I did not. I joined them in going up to the attic to check it out. When we arrived in the attic, we did see a ball on the floor, but it was not moving.

Then we did some EVP work and asked for more signs of a presence. When I reviewed the audio at home, there was nothing on the recorders. Before we left the attic, I asked for any of the spirits to move the ball one more time. For a few seconds, we all thought that the ball started to move. Were we seeing something paranormal? No, unfortunately not. It was just a loose floor board. But what cause Beth and Josh to hear the ball bouncing earlier? Don't have an answer yet.

As we made our way back down to the master bedroom, josh said that he heard a little girls laugh come from the playroom. I entered the playroom and checked it out. I did not get anything on the recorder nor did I hear anything with my ears. I did get the unusual smell of lilacs. This is unusual because there are no flowers on the property and none of the women were wearing perfume. Was this one of the Eldred girls making contact? Not sure, but where did that smell come from?

As we stood outside the playroom door, the three of us all heard footsteps coming up the stairs. The steps got louder as they reached the top of the stairs. I could not see anyone standing at the top of the stairs, but I know that someone was there. The steps stopped for a brief moment, then went down the hall to one of the children's room. We kept a video camera on the sound, but the video showed nothing. The steps were caught on the audio recorder. The steps then started back towards the steps. The steps then stopped again at the top of the stairs. The three of us got this eerie feeling that whatever was there, stopped to look at us. The steps then made their way down the stairs again. This got our blood pumping. But who was is? Our only thought was that it had to be Mr. Eldred due to the heaviness of the steps.

The time was about two in the morning when the rest of the group returned from the graveyard. The three of us went outside to the bonfire to warm up and to talk with others. While at the fire, on lady said that she saw some movement in the upper left hand bedroom window. This window belonged to Emma's room. Josh and I went back into the house and up to Emma's room. We did not see or experience anything unusual. Josh and I joined the other outside by the fire one more time to go over what we had experienced in the house. We informed them of the footsteps and the sound of the bouncing ball. The group was disappointed, because they had nothing at the cemetery.

At three in the morning, Loren and Kelly told us that the investigation was over. This was an overnight investigation, so we were allowed to sleep on the ground. Those who chose to sleep outside were instructed to stay out of the house. Those who were sleeping inside the house (me) had to pick our spots. We had to bring our own sleeping gear since the house was empty of all furniture. When I got inside, I decided (not very wisely I might add) to sleep on the first floor in the family room. Why do I say not wisely? The only roomy area in the family room was right under on of the windows. I froze my butt off. However, it wasn't just the cold that kept me awake. There was something or someone else in the room with me.

As I was on the floor trying to get comfortable and warm (this is why I hate camping), I could hear heavy boot steps walking on the floor in my room. I would pop my head up to see if it was one of the other members of the group, but I could not see anyone. Then I would drift off to sleep for about ten or fifteen minutes, when the boot sounds would start up again. This time, I got up and looked around the room. After seeing nothing in the room, I went out and searched the rest of the floor. The only thing that I found, were the other people in the group fast asleep. As I walked back to my sleeping area, I saw a shadow move in the den. Remember, this is the room where I caught the door move on video. I checked out the den, but had nothing happen to me. I laid down to sleep and heard the boot steps one last time. This time I heard them walk out of the family room and towards the front door. It was dead (pardon the pun) silent after that, and I was able to fall asleep at four in the morning.

At seven in the morning, Loren came around and woke us up. I told him about the boot steps that I heard, and we theorized that it might have been Mr. Eldred checking on us. I gathered my things, packed up the car, thanked MCGH, and got on the road at eight in the morning. This one was a good time (minus the goof). It far out weighed the Opry House case. I had some good personal experiences, plus caught a good piece of video. If you would ever like to tag along with MCGH, please visit their website at www.bumpinthenight.net or search American Ghost Society.

CHAPTER 15: BEYOND REALITY

In November of 2009, I got an opportunity to meet, learn from, and investigate with some of the best paranormal investigators on the planet. I was at the Stanley Hotel in Estes Park, CO for a Beyond Reality Event. The group that headlined the event was The Atlantic Paranormal Society (TAPS) from the television show *Ghost Hunters*. The Stanley Hotel is not only famous for being haunted, but it is also the inspiration for the Steven King novel *The Shining*.

The event started on Friday, but I flew in the night before. I just hung out in my hotel room and got (or tried to) used to the high altitude. This time I didn't get to stay at the Stanley, so I stayed at a hotel about twenty miles away. I had to make the trip each day and night. Then next time I did the Beyond Reality at the Stanley, I stayed there, but more on that later. I arrived at the Stanley at noon, even though I couldn't check in for the event until three in the afternoon. I walked around the hotel, took a few pictures, listened to the tour guides talk about the Stanley, and just got acquainted with the area.

As I was sitting in the hotel lobby (mainly looking at the women), I would see some of the TAPS members walk by. I will admit to being a little star struck. I see these people on television every week and now I'm going to be hanging with them. Probably the best sight that I had was seeing Kris William and Amy Bruni walk by. You should have seen the smile on my face. I also met a few other paranormal groups and did a lot of networking.

At 3pm, it was time to check in for the event. Britt Griffith from TAPS and his wife Holly were in charge of this. He told us to form a line, have identification ready (if applicable), and collect our badges for the weekend. The badges were two different colors, blue and maroon. I was given a maroon badge. This means that I would be investigating on Saturday night. After receiving my badge, I started to mingle with more of the other guests. To my amazement, I met another Minnesotan. His name is Adam Brody. Adam is a professional comic and a paranormal investigator on the side. He was there to help as one of the Master of Ceremonies (MC). I then picked up my schedule for the weekend and signed up for some of the classes that were going to be taught. To tell you I was excited would be an understatement.

After a dinner break, it was time for the meet and greet. This is where you could meet the TAPS members and get autographs and pictures with them. Yes, I marked out and got autograph pictures. Before that happened, we were treated to a live video feed from Rhode Island. It was from Jason Hawes (co-founder of TAPS). He could not be there due to being sick. He did say hello and gave us some tips on investigating and told us a few things to look for while investigating. This was nice to see. The TAPS members who were there were, Britt, Grant Wilson (co-founder of TAPS and cool guy), Kris (HOT), and Amy (HOT!!!).

I arrived back at the Stanley at noon the next day. My first piece of business was to attend a class called *Psychology of the Paranormal*. This class was taught by Jeff Belanger. Jeff is a paranormal author, investigator, and web television personality. His web television show is called *30 Odd Minutes*. It is a great show and I recommend it to everyone. Jeff likes to bring a more light hearted and funny approach to the paranormal. In his class, I learned how legends and folklore can influence someone's perception of a "haunted" location. We also got to see examples of false positives. False positives are things that can be explained, but look real. He shared some of his own stories, clips of his web show, and examples of evidence and non evidence.

His how covers all aspects of the paranormal. He tells you about ghosts, aliens, Bigfoot, vampires, monsters, and all kinds of psychic phenomena. This class was very entertaining and educational. After the class, I spoke with Jeff for a bit and got my picture taken with him. I also love reading his books. I own five of them including *The Investigators Guide to Haunted Places* and *Picture Yourself Legend Tripping*. They teach you where some haunted locations are, some background of why some places might be haunted, and a few how to tips. These books are very worth the time to read and you should go out and get them. There you go Jeff, free plug!

After a twenty minute break, I took my next class. This class was about how your brain works and how it registers things that are paranormal. The guy who taught this class told us about the nerve endings in the brain and eyes. I really didn't learn much in this class and it wasn't anything to write home about. This was more of a high school science lesson than anything else. I don't even know why I took it. Moving on!

We then had an hour to kill before the dinner and auction. I spent it mingling with some of the other guests. After the break, we gathered in this large dining room. I was seated at a back table with some other investigators and one special guest. Joining our table was the Stanley Hotel's resident Jack Nicholson impersonator. "Jack" was a cool guy and never broke character while at the table. He would tell us stories of the Stanley and the fact that he even hears the strange footsteps. It was cool. The auction that they held was to raise money for Multiple Sclerosis. I have a cousin that has it, so I was willing to give. However, I was going for a certain prize.

The prize that I wanted was the seat between Grant Wilson and Britt Griffith. I was unfortunately out bid by this guy who I think had a crush on Grant. He wouldn't leave Grant alone all night. The final bid for that seat I think was $900. I was disappointed that I didn't get it, but I got the next best thing. I won the seat between Kris Williams and Amy Bruni. I won it with a $200 bid, but I bumped it up to $500. I have the picture to prove it.

At the table, I met the family of Kris and Amy. Amy's mom even took a photo of me for the family album of ghost hunting. That's a personal score. I was also talking with a guy who I think was Amy's brother, about tattoos. Also at the table were Kris Williams and her parents Bob and Diane. They were very nice people and wanted to know about me. I was a little shy because I was sitting between these two hot women that I watch on television. It took a bit to break me out of my shell, but they did it.

Once I broke out of the shell, we started to talk about some of the past shows that they did. Then, once Bob found out that I was a wrestler, he wanted to hear stories. Amy's brother was a wrestling fan too, so he wanted to hear stories too. I think I was earning points with the family. I told them some of the funny stories that I had with some past tag partners including the one where one of my partners walked into a store and wanted to buy women's underwear. Yes, you had to be there.

We all talked at the table for about two hours. The whole time I was sitting there talking, I kept thinking one thing. I see these people on television every week and now I am sharing a table with them. This was a great experience and I will never forget it.

When the dinner was over, it was time to relax a bit before the investigation started. I went outside to get a little air, when Bob came up to me to talk some more. We talked for about twenty minutes and then I went inside to talk with Grant. I was able to get my picture taken with him and ask him some advice on what to do if a client does want to believe your findings. He just told me to be respectful and honest. People are going to believe what they want. Most people will be relieved to hear that there is nothing paranormal in their home or business. However, there are those who are 100% convinced that something is there and they want you to believe it too. I was honored that he was willing to talk with me and pose for the picture. He is a great guy.

On Sunday, it was more classes on demonology and religious things. I wanted to take these classes because, wait for it, I wanted to see what the "Jesus Freaks" had to say about the paranormal. It pretty much ended up being what I expected. Everything was a demon or a bad entity. There was never any other explanation to them. In my opinion, all this guy (who is a "expert" in demons) was doing was blowing smoke at us. There were some people who were believing his every word. I felt very sorry for them. There was one thing that he covered that did interest me. That being one of the most famous cases of exorcism. The case of Annleise Michel.

Anna, as I will call her, was a German girl (not bad looking either) who was "possessed" by an evil force. She was a devote Catholic, so that should tell you something right there. She would do weird things like sleeping naked on the floor while it was the middle of winter. She did this to "atone for other people's sins". Sorry, but she is too good looking of a girl to be going down this path. In 1969, it was found that Anna was suffering from Epilepsy. This is a condition in the brain that causes seizures and hallucinations. While in high school, she would experience some of these symptoms. She also began to hear voices in her head that told her that she "was damned". She was also suffering from depression and thoughts of suicide. Her behavior would become strange as well. She would often rip off her clothes, eat coal, and lick up her own urine.

In 1975 (Hey, that's the year I was born), when Anna was 23, and old woman who would accompany her at times, felt she was possessed because she wouldn't drink from the "holy" fountain. This same woman would sell it to the local priests that Anna was possessed because she diverted her eyes from a cross. Little did this woman "forget" to mention, that the cross was made of silver and that this cross was outside of the home. Meaning, the sun glared off the cross and into her eyes. You would divert your eyes too.

From here, the exorcisms started. The whole time these happened, doctors and psychiatrists would try to give Anna medical care. She would refuse it all. Her parents, who also believed that she was possessed, must have been short minded too. They didn't want doctors coming to her aid at all. They wanted the church to take of the problem. She would also refuse all food and water during this ordeal. These exorcisms lasted for ten months with 67 performed in all. In the end, none of them worked. Sadly, Anna died on July 1st, 1976 at the age of 23.

The official medical cause of death was malnutrition and dehydration. Those in the "Jesus World" rule the death as "murder by demonic force". I personally agree with the medical report. I believe that her epileptic attacks became too much for her and she slowly killed herself. It is sad and very unfortunate. If she and her family would have let the doctors treat her, I believe that she would be alive to this day. I do not believe it had anything to do with demons.

After that class was over, it was time for a small break. The next course that I took was on Electronic Voice Phenomena (EVP). This was taught by world renowned EVP specialists Mark and Debbie Constantino. They are a husband and wife team from the west coast. You can tell that they are married couple, because they argue and tell each other off at times. One of the funniest things I have ever seen. They have been on numerous television shows and radio programs.

The class was a brief one lasting only fifty minutes. It consisted of the different EVP's that they have collected over the years. Some of them were funny and a few of them were creepy (if they are real). I did learn how to use different question techniques and how to use the audio recorders in a better way. One thing I found very helpful, they taught me the difference between real EVP and just garbled noise. It made me go back and review some of my EVPs. I only have to throw out 3 of them. They are a real nice couple and I was glad to learn from them.

We then broke for dinner and side auction for ghost hunting equipment. I did the dinner, but not the auction. After the break, it was time for the question and answer session with the TAPS members. They talked about their favorite cases, places to investigate and what their dream case would be. It turns out that Kris's dream case is the grave of Jim Morrison. Apparently she has the hots for a dead guy. It's ok, I have always had a thing for Audrey Hepburn.

That's all that happened in 2009. Before I get to the investigation, I am going to briefly talk about the event I attended in 2010. It was also in November, but this time I got to stay at the Stanley. I stayed on the fourth floor of the main hotel. This is the most haunted floor. I stayed in room 417, which is just down the hall from the most haunted room 401. I will cover that in the next chapter.

The classes were the same and it was just a refresher course. The only difference was the ghost equipment course that Britt Griffith taught. I learned what cameras are the best to use without going overboard on cost. I learned how to examine the still photos of ghosts. Meaning, what is a pure anomaly and what is a strand of hair, camera strap, and the like. I also had a chance to talk with Jeff Belanger a little more this time. He gave me some advice about book writing and how to get the message of my stories out there. I am again very thankful to him.

I met a few new people at this one. After the previous year's event, I was more open to people and networked a lot. I met K.J. McCormick, Dustin Pari, and new TAPS member Adam Barry this year. They were really cool people and I was amazed on how laid back Dustin is. One thing that I was surprised by was the fact that Amy remembered me from the previous year. With all the people she meets at these events, I was honored. But, then again, who can forget this face. There was not an auction dinner, but a silent auction for items. I won a crew pass from the 2010 Halloween Live event that TAPS did. I got it autographed by Amy and Britt.

I had more fun this time around than last time. I think because I was more relaxed. I had elk meat also for the first time while I was there. I ate at the hotel restaurant and had the elk meatloaf. It was the second best meatloaf I ever had. What is the best? Well my mom's of course. I am so glad that I did these events. Not only did I learn a lot, but I also got to meet great people and hang with celebrities. I truly had the time of my life.

CHAPTER 16:
THE INVESTIGATION 2009 & 2010

Ok, you are all wondering (or at least I hope you are) what I caught during the investigations. First I would like to say that this was an absolute thrill to investigate with the TAPS crew. This was a dream come true for me. I am going to talk about the 2009 investigation first. The Saturday group (which I was in), met inside the concert hall. After a brief discussion on how things were going to go, we were split into groups. I was placed in a group of about 15 people. Each member of TAPS were in charge of a specific area of the hotel. Grant would be floating between all the areas to talk and give his advice.

My first location was the basement of the hotel. Amy Bruni was in charge of this spot. Nothing happened at all while we were in this area. There were too many people walking around and making noise, so I threw out all my audio from this area. I then just switch to my video, and again found nothing of any significance. Some of the other people were using their K-2 Meters to find EMF readings. The problem was, all of the K-2 Meters were flying off the charts. This was due to the rock in the basement being made of limestone. Limestone is a conductor of EMF Fields. So, those tools were useless here.

After about 30 minutes, Grant showed up in the basement. We joked around with him and he gave us some good investigation tips.

He shared his stories from the hotel and about the little girl's voice that was caught in the basement. He went over the false positives that limestone can create with the K-2, and to look at every possible explanation before labeling something paranormal. When I got home, I reviewed the video, but sadly caught nothing. However, a free instructional from Grant was very cool.

The next stop on the investigation was the Concert Hall. This one was lead by Kris Williams. The claims of activity down here were hearing footsteps and seeing the apparition of a woman who froze to death. I will talk about this woman later in the 2010 investigation. I positioned myself in the upstairs projection and control room. I sat there videotaping the others on the main floor do a K-2 session. The others would ask any spirit to make its presence known by lighting up the lights on the K-2. We were in there for 40 minutes and the K-2 did not light up once. While I was in the room, I kept hearing what sounded like someone walking behind me. Unfortunately, my camera did not catch it.

I then left that room and went down into the sub level of the Hall. I searched all of the rooms, but did not experience anything unusual. Some of the other guests said that they felt the presence of this woman. However, there was no evidence of this. Just like with the basement, I reviewed the tape when I got home. The tape showed nothing.

After a brief break, we were off to the Manor House. The Manor House is a side building of the hotel. The room that we were going to investigate was Room 1302. This is the room where Grant had a table move on him while he was changing a tape. Mark and Debbie Constantino were the heads of this room. This was going to be a 100% EVP session. I sat in a chair and video recorded the entire session. Throughout the time in the room, many people claimed that they caught EVP after asking questions. We would play back the audio live in the room. I did not hear anything that did not sound like garbled noise. Mark and Debbie tried their hardest to get me to hear the voices, but I just wasn't getting it. After someone planted the words in my head, I could hear it. The only way I heard it was through the power of suggestion, so I don't know if it was a real EVP or if it was nothing. It was cool to be there though.

After another small break, it was back into the main hotel and the 4th floor. The room we went to was Room 401. This room is named after Lord Dunraven. Lord Dunraven is the man who owned the land that the hotel is on before the Stanley's bought it. The claims of activity in here, are women getting felt up by unseen hands, the closet door opens by its own, and disembodied voices. Britt Griffith was in charge of this room. We did not come in contact with Lord Dunraven or anything paranormal, but did have one interesting thing happen.

I was sitting in a chair and Britt was on the floor with his back against the wall. Between the two of us was a ironing board that we had leaning against the door. As we were asking for a sign of any spirits presence, we noticed the ironing board jump a bit. We had all thought, at the time, that the spirit in the room had made contact. We asked for it to do it again, but it did not. Was it paranormal? Unfortunately no, we found an explanation.

Here is what happened. Britt got up and said that he was going to check outside in the hallway to make sure no one was out there. Well, there was someone out there and this person was drunk. I don't just mean tipsy, I mean DRUNK! The guy mumbled something to Britt, and after some constant repeating, we were able to ascertain that the guy was looking for someone named Chris. Britt told the guy that "Chris" was one floor down. We all got a good laugh out of this. Ok, you had to be there for it. Again, nothing paranormal caught on tape, unless you count the drunk.

The last stop on the 2009 investigation was the Steven King Room or Room 217. He was staying in this room when he experienced some form of paranormal activity to inspire him to write *The Shining*. The claims of activity here were the sounds of children laughing, footsteps in the room, and the apparition of a former house maid. The couple in charge of this room were from the west coast. I did not know who they were. All I know that the woman had very large breasts. Yes, I was looking.

Nothing was really happening in the room during our 40 minutes stay. I did however hear something happening out in the hallway. To me, it sounded like there was an argument going on. I mentioned it to the others in the room, but no one else said that they heard it. Once I heard it again, I opened up the room door. Once the door was open, the "argument" stopped. I then closed the door and we continued with our investigation. After about four minutes, I heard the argument again. This time, one of the other guys heard it too. We went out in the hallway and listened at the doors of the other rooms. We did this to make sure we weren't hearing a television or just two people. Again, the sound had stopped. I heard the argument one more time and the same guy who heard it before, accompanied me in the hallway again. This time, we did find the cause of the sound. One of the vents by the door of room 217 is right above the gift shop. The gift shop had its radio still on and I was hearing the radio. Another one shot down.

As far as the 2009 investigation goes, it was cool to be with the TAPS crew. However, I have to go by the video/audio that I shot. As far as I was concerned, there was nothing really there. Others had experiences, but I did not. But, as many in the field have said, never judge a place on one visit. So, now we go to the 2010 investigation. This one was more interesting and a lot more fun. Ready? Here we go.

Again we were split into groups. The group I was got to be the first group to investigate the Administrative Building. The claims in this building were that of a spirit of a little child that likes to play. Also, some of the workers have said that a former employee named Ray is seen in there from time to time. The head of this building would be Amy Bruni. A few of the others in my group went up to the second floor to look for Ray. I stayed in the meeting room with Amy. Amy started doing the flashlight test. I have seen this done many times on their television shows. Now, I was going to see it with my own eyes. To say I was a bit pumped would be an understatement.

Amy set the flashlights on the table and we asked for any spirit to make its presence known. After a few minutes of no action, Amy said that she would give the spirit a treat if it would make its presence known. In my mind, I was wondering what treat would she give, if the spirit was Ray. I know what I would have asked for! Hey. Amy is HOT! Amy asked if the spirit was the little child. She said that she would give the child candy if it would light the flashlight up. I have the whole thing on video, but after she said that, the flashlight lit up. Then, one of the other women in the group asked the child to turn off the light. The light flickered for a few seconds and then shut off. I spent about 45 minutes here and saw this event happen six times. It was amazing.

I did go upstairs for a few minutes, but did not experience anything. I am not going to talk about room 217, because nothing happened while we were there. Dustin Pari was in charge to 217. He did share some of his stories from being on the show and being overseas. I am also going to skip the basement. Britt was in charge here. Some of the other people in the group said that they hear the voice of a female in the basement. I was able to debunk this due to finding another air vent that led to the 1st floor lobby. One thing to keep in mind, when doing these investigations, sound does travel.

Now we go to room 1302 in the Manor House. K.J. was in charge of this one. We were looking for the spirit of a man who likes to get "comfortable" with the single ladies. Also we were told of footsteps, and the table that moved on Grant. Again, we got some good interaction with the flashlight. We got the spirit to answer question by turning the light on and off. We even asked if it found any of the ladies in the group good looking. It turned the light on strong. It was thinking along the same lines as I was.

We then moved to the main hotel and to the famous room 401. New TAPS member Adam Berry was in charge of this. We tried real hard to get Lord Dunraven to make his presence known. We asked for knocks, for him to move something, and I even used my fake British accent to get him to come out. The only thing that would happen was the flashlight would go on and off. However, this time it wouldn't do it in a "smart" way. Meaning it wouldn't really interact, it would just randomly go on and off. The only thing that we found odd, was the room got about three degrees cooler while we were in there. This is odd, because there were 11 of us in there. You would think the temp should go up. No explanation for this one.

On Sunday night, I got to investigate the Concert Hall. The hall was not available for us who had the Saturday night investigation due to a wedding being there. After the Q&A session on Sunday, there was a fifty minute window for us to investigate the hall. My main focus here was to try and come in contact with Lucy. Adam Berry, his friend Ben, and I were in this dressing room investigating. Inside the dressing room was a small bathroom. Adam, Ben, and I all heard the bathroom door closing, but nothing was on camera. Again, I have no explanation how this could be. All three of us heard it and we know it was from inside that room. Was this a residual sound that Lucy made years ago while she was alive? Could be. I will label this one paranormal since I do not have an explanation and there were witnesses.

SO, what are my overall thoughts about The Stanley and Beyond Reality? I enjoyed every minute I was there. I know I have said that many times before, but it is true. I was able to explain away certain things and see things that I can not explain. Is the hotel haunted? I can not say either way. I would like to bring BPIMN here sometime and have to place to ourselves. Maybe then, I could have an answer for you. I will tell you right now that this is a beautiful place in a beautiful part of the country. If you ever get the chance to visit Colorado, take a trip up to Estes Park and the Stanley Hotel. Ghost hunter or not, it is a great experience that everyone should enjoy.

CHAPTER 17: MY TWO GRANDPAS

This deals with what happened in 2009 when I returned from Colorado. My dad picked me up at the airport and as we drove, we talked about my trip. Out of the blue, my dad asked if I could take him to a hospital in Minneapolis. Thinking that there was something wrong with him, I asked if he was alright. Dad told me that he was fine, but all the family was there for Grandpa Ray. I knew that grandpa wasn't doing well and that when the family gathers, that it's not a good thing. Dad had told me that the doctors were saying that grandpa wouldn't make it through the night. It was a very sinking feeling, but I kept saying to myself "we have been hearing that for the last year".

IS there a reason that I am talking about my Grandpa Ray? Yes there is and it does have something to do with the paranormal. More on that later. Let me give you some back ground on my Grandpa Ray. Raymond A. Prochaska was born in May of 1922. He grew up on a farm and became a farmer after school. In the 1940's, he joined the US Navy and served for a few years. After the service, he came back to Minnesota and married my Grandmother Dorothy Laban. He stayed in the farming business and drove a truck to support his family. All together, Grandpa and Grandma had six kids with my mom being the oldest. He lived is life in Montgomery, MN. When I was born, he had retired and spent his time working in the garage. He would be fixing cars, our bikes, or just putzing around.

Ray was a big wrestling fan as well. When I was young, I can remember watching wrestling with him when I stayed overnight at the grandparents house. So, I think there might have been a little pride in him when I turned professional. I can remember him sitting with my family in the crowd when I had my debut pro match. He would came and see me wrestle occasionally when I was in the area. He would do this even when he wasn't feeling the best. After he had his first stroke, he stopped coming to the shows. He would still like to talk with me about wrestling however. He would have another stroke a few years later and the conversations would get more difficult. He knew what was going on and could understand you, but had trouble talking. I was feeling really bad.

The last time I saw him was Easter of 2009. He was in bad shape and never left the bedroom. He was having stomach problems and his legs were too weak to move. When those of us were getting ready to leave, we went into the bedroom to say goodbye. It was difficult for me to see a family member in that condition. That is why I do not like to visit family in hospitals or nursing homes. I can't just stand there looking at them and know that there is nothing I can do for them. Anyway, I said goodbye to him and wished for him to get better. Little did I know, that this was the last time I would see him alive.

Ray had been in and out of the hospital numerous times during 2009. In October and November, things took a turn for the worse. He got a nasty infection and his immune system was too weak to fight it off. The doctors pumped him full of antibiotics, it stopped the infection, but it did damage his fingers and toes. Grandpa stayed in that hospital for a week and a half. So much for going that night huh doc? I knew my grandpa wasn't going down without a fight. However, he just didn't get better. After the doctors did all they could do, they granted his final wish. He wanted to be moved to the nursing home where my grandma Dorothy was. After the move, his heath took a major downward spiral. He died on November 20th, 2009. He was 87 years old.

I was sitting in my security office at work when I got the call from my brother. When I saw his number on my cell phone, I knew why he was calling. Emotions are funny at times. You prepare yourself for the news, you know its coming, but it still hits you like a truck. My brother's voice was very shaky, so I knew he was crying. I asked him if mom wanted all of us down at the nursing home. He told me that mom did want me there, so I found coverage at work and then headed down to the nursing home. I only went down there because mom wanted me there. I knew that there was nothing else I could do. As much as I wanted to, I couldn't turn back time. As I drove down, all the memories of grandpa raced through my head. I just couldn't believe he was gone.

When I arrived at the nursing home, my brother met me at the door. He led me to the waiting area where that family had gathered. After talking with a few of my cousins, I went to where mom was. She was out in the hall out side of grandpa's room. I talked with mom and grandma for a bit, when mom asked me a very strange question. She asked me "Do you want to go in and see him?". After the shock elapsed, I said no. Call me stupid (all together now), but like I said, I do not like seeing my family like that. Mom then told me that I would see him at the funeral. She was right, but then it would seem more real.

I went back to the waiting area to sit with the rest of the family. When the funeral director arrived, he sat with the family and asked some questions. He would ask grandma when she wanted the wake to be, funeral, clothing for grandpa, and what not. It was great entertainment watching the director and grandma talk. You see, the director speaks very softly and grandma is very hard of hearing. So, every time the director would ask grandma a question, grandma would yell "WHAT?". Then the director would whisper a bit louder. The exchange went on for about twenty five minutes. You could tell that the director was starting to get frustrated. I found the whole thing hilarious.

In the end, mom and my uncles decided to discuss the matters the next day. Grandma was taken back to her room and the director went to his car to get the body bag. After coming back in, the director and my uncles Rod and Gordy went to get my grandpa. After saying our goodbyes, everyone left except for me. This is where it kind of goes to the paranormal side. Something inside my head told me to stay.

In my mind, it wasn't real until I saw him get wheeled out by the director. It sounds morbid I know, but I needed to see it. I knew it was coming because the nursing staff went from room to room closing the doors. Then after a few minutes, I saw him get wheeled out to the hearse. It was at that moment that the tough guy in me went away and the tears started to flow. I could not control it, the emotion hit me very hard. Here is where it gets more paranormal. As I was sitting in the chair crying, I hear a voice in my right ear. The voice was very close to what my grandpa Ray sounded like. The voice told me not to worry and that everything is alright. I looked up to see if anyone was around, but I could not see anyone. Was it grandpa Ray telling me he was ok? I don't know, but it did make me feel better. I said my final goodbye to him four days later at the cemetery. Raymond Prochaska May 1922 – November 2009.

Now Grandpa Ray was the only one that I ever knew. That's because my other grandfather Lawrence Dorn died 12 years before I was born. However, I am convinced that I met him once. Grandpa Lawrence died in 1963 of what I believe was a brain aneurism. Not sure as to what the main cause of it was, but I know he did drink. This is the main reason why I refuse to drink alcohol. I have only seen two pictures of him. From what I understand, he wasn't photographed very much because he didn't like it. I was told the only way to take his picture is you had to catch him when he wasn't looking. From what I could tell, he was a good looking guy. So that explains where I get it from. And, from my dad of course.

This is why I think I met him. Back in 2003, I was dating this girl who had a hair appointment in New Prague. As much as I really wanted to stay at the salon with her (sarcasm), I told her that I was going to visit my grandparents on my dad's side. I told her that I would be back in about 20 minutes. The cemetery where they are buried is on the west side of town. Ironically enough, it is located one block from the house where they lived. When I pulled into the cemetery, I was wondering how I would find their stone. All I had to go on was a picture of their stone that was taken in 1982. The cemetery had tripled since then. I must have circled the graves about three times. I knew I was in the right area, because I was on one of the drive paths. So, on a whim, I got out of the car and asked for help.

I stood outside my car and asked my grandfather to show me where his stone was. At that moment, a black bird flew out of a tree and landed on a gravestone. The thought that went through my head was "There is no way that could be their stone". I walked to the stone slowly, because I was expecting the bird to fly at my face and peck it off. As I got closer to the stone, the bird just looked at me. I then asked the bird if this was my grandparent's stone. It then took two small steps at me and squawked at me. When I walked to the front of the stone, I was surprised to find that it was their stone. This was amazing. I looked at the bird and for some reason said "thank you grandpa". The bird squawked again and then flew off. Was this Grandpa Dorn helping me out? I would like to think so. If not, then it is one of the strangest coincidences of all time. I am dedicating this chapter to my two grandfathers. They were both good men and in a way, helped make me who I am today.

CHAPTER 18:
SKEPTICS, PSYCHICS & CYNICS

I am going to take this time to talk to you about four types of people you will meet in this field. These types are believers, skeptics, cynics, and psychics. These people can be both good for your investigations and bad. I have run into all of these types and will tell you a bit about them in this short chapter and some of my experiences with them.

The first one that I would like to cover are the believers. You might think that believers are the best thing to an investigator. Well, you would be wrong. Granted, if people didn't believe, we wouldn't doing this. As long as they are level headed and open to hearing you out, they are great. However, you will run into those believers that will over react when things go bump. Around 12% to 15% want their house or business to be haunted and won't listen to anything of the contrary.

The point that I am making when it comes to believers being bad are that they could tend to drive you away from doing the investigation. When BPIMN does an investigation, we do an interview with the client first. I might have mentioned that in a previous chapter, oh well. You sit there and listen to everything they say to you. Sometimes, they tell you stories that are so far fetched, so you would believe their every word. They will add things to their stories to spice them up a bit. I even had one interview where the client explained all of the activity in their home. The problem was, that the described the movie *Poltergeist* to me. They even went as far as to add the coffins in the pool.

Basically, you need to be able to read people and weed through the crap that some of them want to feed you. Again, most of the bad ones just want the notoriety of having a haunt. It makes them feel special. However, there as those believers who are genuine. These people are the ones that have experienced things and are asking you for help. These people keep their calm and explain what is happening without going into over the top detail. They also will be more accepting of your findings. Most of the time, they just want answers. If you can find logical explanations for the activity, then they will have their nerves eased and can get on with their lives. On the other side, if you do have evidence of a haunting/activity, then they will listen to your results and take the advice on how to advance with the situation.

No matter how you deal with it, you need to be professional and honest with them. In the end, they are going to take away for your investigation what they want. Whatever happens, do not let them sway your results. Never second guess yourself or your findings in order to fit their needs.

The next group that I will talk about are the Skeptics. I love having these people around. Plus, it helps if you and the rest of your team are skeptics. Skeptics are people who don't really believe in the paranormal, but are at least open to the possibility that something is out there that is hard to explain. When reviewing footage, they will help you determine if there are logical explanations for the activity. They can also give you an even further outside view of the situation. They also will help you weed through any crap that some clients will throw at you. There have been times when a client said some weird things and a few investigators were believing it. The skeptic jumped in and asked some follow up questions and was able to see through the crap. These people are very level headed and helpful for all points of the investigation. If a skeptic asks to come on an investigation, please bring them with. You'll be glad you did.

Now we come to the lesser of the bunch. These people are Cynics. To me, these people are just a pain in the ass. Cynics don't/won't believe in the paranormal no matter what. A cynic could have a full body apparition form right in front of them, slap them in the face, and still deny that it happened. They will go through every possible explanation for activity caught on film, but unlike skeptics, after all the explanations have been exhausted, they will say that it was trickery on your part. You can not convince these people no matter what you do. So my advice to you is to not even try.

Cynics will also try to tear apart all of your video and audio recordings. They will say things like, "video cameras are meant to record things that are there and not things that aren't. You are putting those voices on there by speaking real soft". Yes, I have had these things said to me. When it comes to EMF recordings, they will say that you are causing the recordings and not a spirit. Their whole reason for being there is to prove you a fraud. No amount of evidence will make a cynic think twice. To them, anything caught on video or audio was faked by you to take advantage of people. The best way to deal with these people is to just keep doing what you do. Just ignore them.

Now we come to some of the most wacky people on the planet. Who am I talking about? Psychics! Some paranormal groups use them and have had success. Other groups, like BPIMN, do not for two reasons. First, we are a scientific group who documents its findings on video and audio. Second, you only have the word of the psychic to go off of.

Psychics tend to only go off what they are feeling. They will tell you that they feel a presence in the corner of the room. So, you point your cameras in the corner with the hope of catching something. In my opinion, you have a better chance of catching belly button lint that anything paranormal. EVP sessions are hit and miss as well. They will sit in a chair and claim that they are having a conversation with a little girl. But, when you play the recording back, all you hear is the psychic's voice.

Now, don't even get me started on their so called "channeling". This is where the psychic will allow a spirit to enter their body and use it as a way of communication. Then, they will start to speak how "they" think the spirit would sound. They will use terms from a certain period of time and make it sound like the spirit is talking to you. To me and others in BPIMN, this is all just a show.

Psychics will also do readings of people of things. But, you have to ask yourself some questions before consulting a psychic. First, if they are psychic, why do they need to as you questions about your past or your family? Also, why do they need a personal artifact in order to do a reading? If they truly are psychic, shouldn't they already know the answers? Shouldn't they know what you are going to say before you say it? These are questions that many have been asking for some time.

There is a difference between psychic and sensitives. A sensitive is someone who, unlike psychics, can't see or hear spirits. They can however, feel when they are near. We do use a sensitive on very rare occasions. His name is Justin. He can feel the energy of a spirit. Like I said, he can't see or hear them, but can determine if the spirit is male or female. We all have some type of sensitive ability. Here's what I mean. Have you ever gone somewhere, like a bar or parking lot, and had that feeling that something bad was about to happen? Or, you stand next to someone and you just get the feeling that this person isn't nice? That is having sensitive ability. Justin just can tune into it a bit further.

Getting back to psychics, you just need to be careful when using them. A large number of the population have preconceived notions about them. Yours truly is one of them. There are way too many frauds out there and that affects your credibility. Just take what they tell you with a grain of salt and stay true to your video and audio findings. Basically, make sure all of the people in your group and level headed and those you are dealing with are not trying to pull one over on you.

CHAPTER 19: HAUNTED IOWA INN

I got through the Christmas holiday and new year without anything exciting happening. I did a lot of wrestling and work. I took December off from ghost hunting due to it being the holiday season and I wanted to be closer to the family. I also needed to catch up on a lot of video and audio recordings that I had collected. When I finally got caught up with everything, I received a call from an Inn in southern Iowa. They were known for having activity and wanted us to come in and do an investigation. I read up on it and found that other groups have had some success gathering evidence. So I made the call to the team to get ready for another investigation. Well, the time off was nice, but back to work.

The phone call came from an Inn in Bentensport, IA. Bentensport is located in extreme south central Iowa. After exchanging a few emails and phone calls, we settled on the date of February 6th, 2010. The team all met in Albert Lea, MN before making the 6 hour trip. The trip went by fast due to Derek and I telling wrestling stories. It made the six hour trip seem like two hours. You should have seen Mark's face after hearing some of the stories. At one time, I thought he was going to pee his pants after hearing them. It was great.

When we arrived, Sarah met us at the front door. We were introduced to the owners Joy and Chuck. They were a nice couple and had owned the Inn for some time. They took us on a tour and showed us where the hot spots of activity are. We were also given a brief history of the building and the surrounding area. After the tour, minus Eric (he arrived late), we left to go to dinner and discuss the plan of action for the night.

While at dinner, people looked at us weird due to us wearing our BPIMN shirts. After a while, some people came up to us and asked us if we were checking out the Inn. When we said yes, like so many other times, the stories came out of things that they had seen. They were all nice people, but it was a little creepy being very small town USA. When we returned from dinner, Eric had met us at the Inn. We gave him a brief catch up and he was ready to dig in. Now, it was time for equipment set up. Mark and set up the static (stationary) night vision camera in room 7. This was the room where the only murder took place in the Inn. The rest of the Inn would be covered with hand held cameras and audio recorders. Also, we had a standard EMF meter and a K-2 meter. After set up was complete, we split up into groups of two.

Before I get into the investigation, I would like to cover some of the history for you. Here is the story of room 7. This is the room where a man named Mr. Knapp was killed. In 1860, Mr. Knapp had checked into the Inn and left to go to a local bar. After a night of heavy drinking, he returned to the Inn and went up to his room. Well, he was too drunk to remember which one was his, so he went into a room that looked similar. As he was getting into bed, the man who was in the bed thought he was being robbed. So the man pulled the sword out of his cane and stabbed Mr. Knapp in the heart. So, the man skipped the questioning and went right to the execution. From what we are to believe, the man pleaded self defense and got away with the act. Things were different back then. Today, the man would spend some time in jail.

There are also some of the Inn's former owners that still haunt the place. One of them haunts the third floor sewing room and the other haunts the fireplace on the first floor. There is also the spirit of a doctor in the Inn. During the 1930's, the doctor stayed in room number 5 on the second floor. The room is known as the Doctor

Room and some of his medical tools can still be seen in the room. It is kind of creepy to see these things. He died in the room of Diphtheria in 1940. People have claimed that they hear his footsteps pacing in the room. Back during the Civil War, the Inn was used as a make shift hospital. It was basically for Union Soldiers. The main Union spirit we were told to look for was a man by the name of Harold or Harry. We were told that as many as 200 spirits come and go from the house. The owners said that some of the spirits were recruiters for other spirits to stay at the Inn. If that is true, then that means there is Human Resources in the afterlife.

Now, onto the investigation. Mark and I started in Room 7. Our first order of business was to get an overall feeling of the room. This is done by walking around, snapping pictures, and just listening. After getting the feel of the room, we started an EVP session. In addition to using audio recorders, we placed a K-2 meter on the bed. The first "person" we tried to get in contact with was Mr. Knapp. We asked for signs of his presence by asking for knocks, moving of objects, or touching one of us. Over the course of the first hour and a half, Mr. Knapp did not make any contact. However, someone or should I say something else did.

As I was asking questions to anyone who was in the room with Mark and I, the K-2 meter began to light up. After it had calmed down a bit, I asked the spirit to light it up again. The lights lit up. Then I asked for the spirit to light the lights up when I got to the letter of it's first name. When I got to the letter H, the lights lit up. The lights lit up another two times after that. Once, when I asked if the spirit was a Civil War soldier. The other time was when I asked the spirit was that of Harold. It was kind of amazing to me. I have seen the K-2 meter used on television, but never seen in done in real life. Mark and I then asked Harold if he knew Mr. Knapp, but the lights remained silent. For the next forty minutes, we didn't have any other activity.

As we were ready to wrap up the first session, Mark asked the spirit if the Inn was used as a hospital. The lights lit up again. The lights lit up again when Mark asked, "Did you help some of the wounded". After that, we lost contact with whomever or whatever was in the room with us. The only other thing that happened at this time was that I thought that I heard a young child running down the small hallway. None of our audio recorders caught this, so it goes down as a personal experience.

Down the hall in Room 5 (Doctor's Room), Eric and Tom were doing some EVP work when they started to hear some knocking sounds. Eric said that the knocking sounded like someone was responding in Morse Code. Since he didn't know the code, he couldn't translate it. They both believed that someone was trying to communicate with them. They also said to me that they heard the running of a child down the hall. Again, nothing was caught on video or audio. However, we now have two different groups that heard the same thing. This gives the activity a little bit more credence.

Sarah and Derek were up in the third floor sewing room. The claims of activity here were hearing the sounds of a rocking chair and some disembodied voices. None of our video and audio recorders caught anything, but Sarah and Derek both heard a strange squeaking noise. They also said that they heard what sounded like the ticking of a clock. There were no clocks in the room. Could this have been the sound of the rocking chair? Difficult to say at this point, no explanation.

When the session was over, we took a fifteen minute break. We were able to change tapes in the cameras, batteries in the recorders, and talk about the things that we experienced. When the break was over, I sent Derek & Tom to Room 7, Mark and Eric to a side room to monitor the hallway, and Sarah and I stayed at base command. Sarah and I watched the static camera in Room 7. Mark and Eric had nothing happen to them in the side room. Nor, did they notice anything happen in the hallway. Tom and Derek thought that they heard some footsteps in Room 7, but couldn't track the source. They did have one other odd thing happen to them. While Tom was laying on the bed, he claimed that he felt it shake. He said that it wasn't a violent shake, but enough to feel. Tom said that it happened when he said out loud, "If you don't want me on your bed, give me a signs". After the bed shook, Tom politely got off the bed.

On the first floor, Sarah did have an experience. While we were watching the static camera monitor, she said that she could hear footsteps coming from above us. Well, the room above us was Room 5. I yelled up to the teams to stop what they were doing, so Sarah and I could hear the footsteps more clear. Once all the teams confirmed that they weren't moving, Sarah heard three footsteps. I went upstairs to Room 5, but found nothing. After I returned to the first floor, the teams went back to investigating. Ten minutes later, Sarah heard the footsteps again. But, this time, she heard some scratches along with them. I marked it down and would ask the owners in the morning if they had any problems with rodents. That was the only rational explanation we could come up with for those noises.

We then broke for another fifteen minute break. We talked about the footsteps in the Doctor's Room (Room 5). We changed tapes again and separated again for the third session. Sarah and Eric went to Room 7, Mark and Tom were at base command, and Derek and I went to the third floor sewing room. Tom and Mark said that they heard the scratching noises just one time. They told me that it sounded more like rodents to them. Sarah and Eric didn't have anything happen to them in Room 7. However, Derek and I did have one thing happen.

The two of us were doing an EVP session with the K-2 meter. We got the lights to light up three times. The first time was when I asked if anyone in the room with us. Then I asked the spirit to light up the lights when I reached the letter of it's first name. It lit up when I reached the letter H. When I asked if the spirit's name was Harold, the lights lit up again. The k-2 meter kept silent the rest of the session. Also, we had no other personal experiences in the sewing room.

After the last break was over, we all gathered in Room 7. We did this because we wanted one more try at communicating with Mr. Knapp. We stayed in the room for only 40 minutes, doing EVP and K-2. The only possible evidence that was caught, was captured by

Mark's camera. You hear me ask the rest of the group, "We've been here all night. Do you want to mean it up a bit". After the other say no, there is a deep voice that says "I'd rather not". Otherwise, we not no other paranormal activity happen to us in the room. We did have a funny moment. While doing the EVP session, Tom fell asleep. So, we all sneaked up on him quietly and yell at the top of our lungs. Tom jumped about two feet in the air. That will teach you for falling asleep Tom. We all got a good laugh from it.

We decided that we were all very tired, so we broke down the equipment. After packing up, we went to our rooms for the night. Derek and I stayed (in separate beds), in Room 5, Sarah stayed in Room 6, Tom and Eric stayed in Room 7, and Mark stayed in room 2. Tom, Eric, and Mark had no experiences while they were sleeping. Derek said that for a while, he felt like someone was watching him. I had the felling like things were crawling on my legs. The owners said that the spirits of cats like to jump into bed with you. However, I was able to disprove this by noticing that the blankets shed thin strands of thread. These threads would attach to the hairs on my legs causing the feel of things crawling.

Around five in the morning, Sarah came into our room. She grabbed a blanket and slept on the floor at the foot of the beds that Derek and I were in. This was a bit weird, but I was tired, so I fell asleep. Sarah left the house at 7 in the morning because she had a family function to go to. As she was leaving, she woke me up to tell me that she would explain everything the next day. Well, this is what happened. As she was in bed in Room 6, she kept hearing heavy boot steps walking by the bed. She also said that she felt a few tugs on the blanket. Sarah would ask the spirits to leave her alone, but they kept bothering her. So, she came into our room to at least get some sleep.

We woke up around nine in the morning. We got down to the first floor where Joy and Chuck served us breakfast. The breakfast was not that good. It was blueberry pancakes (yuck), one fried egg, and dried bacon. Needless to say, we stopped for food on the way home. During breakfast, I asked Chuck if they had any problems with rodents. I explained why I was asking and about the footsteps. He said that they don't have rodents and that the sounds we heard was the Doctor pacing in his room. Now, I didn't mention that it was coming from the Doctor's room. Was it really the Doctor? Or, was it a canned response that they had ready? None of us can say for sure.

The overall feeling of the place is that it does have some form of paranormal activity. We are not ready to say it is haunted though. We just had some weird things that we can't explain happen to us. It is a place that we would love to come back to in the future. It is a historic bed and breakfast where you can share history, breakfast, and maybe a room with a ghost.

CHAPTER 20: NEW ORLEANS

We did a few other cases in 2010, but none of them gathered any evidence. Well, nothing that couldn't be explained away that is. So I am going to tell you about the haunted trip to one of the most haunted cities in the United States. The crescent city itself, New Orleans, LA. I have always wanted to go to New Orleans and when Troy Taylor and American Ghost Society (AGS) planned a trip there in June of 2010, I jumped at the chance. I flew down one day earlier, so I could walk the French Quarter and see things. I checked into the Andrew Jackson hotel, which was said to be haunted.

As I was checking in, another couple from the east coast had overheard my questioning of the clerk of the hauntings. The couple asked me if I was a ghost hunter and I said yes. I became an instant celebrity in their eyes. They were asking me about my investigations and all the places that I have been. They then asked if I was investigating the hotel. I said that I would do some poking around, but would not conduct a full investigation. I found out that they were staying in the room across the courtyard from my room. So, I told them that if they experienced anything to let me know and I would do the same for them. They asked me what I was doing in town. I told them that I was here to tour the above ground cemeteries and investigate a haunted mortuary. They asked if they could come with, I told them that it was a private thing for AGS. We said our goodbyes and went our separate ways.

I continued my conversation with the clerk about the hotel being haunted. The clerk said that she never had anything happen to her, but did hear stories from some of the other guests. She said that the only stories are of hearing children laughing and running around the courtyard fountain. This was great news because the fountain was right outside my room door. The time was six in the evening, so after putting my bags in the room, I walked the French Quarter. I walked into a few of the shops to look. The place was wall to wall New Orleans Saints stuff. Now I like the saints, but even I thought it was a bit much. But, whatever works right?

I then went into a voodoo museum. Can't visit New Orleans with out going to one of those. I lucked out, because this one was one I had seen on television. I entered through a very small door that I barely fit through. Once I got the door closed, I turned and had large alligator head staring at me. Not a fan of reptiles. I looked around the small lobby for a bit and then rang the bell on the desk. From the back came with small, white haired man. I talked with him for about five minutes and then paid a fee to tour the museum. I saw old painting of some of the voodoo queens and there were also skulls and other things to look at. To be honest, the television program on the museum was more interesting.

After the tour (which I took by myself) was over, I stopped and talked with the man again. He asked me what I thought about the city and his shop. I told him that it was my first time in New Orleans and the museum was cool. He then asked me if I wanted to buy any spells, herbs, or potions. I told him no, because I wasn't a believer in voodoo and also I don't think it would be good to bring it on the plane home. He laughed at the plane thing, but didn't like that I wasn't a believer. I told him that everyone has their own beliefs and what's good for one isn't good for others. He told me that he would make me a believer before I left the shop. All he needed from me was a drop of my blood. Yeah, I don't like it when doctor's take blood let alone a stranger. I couldn't get out of that shop fast enough.

I then went next door to a shop called The Vampire Boutique. The girl behind the counter was smoking hot. The girl had long black hair and was dressed in an all gothic school girl outfit. Forgive me as I take a second to remember. Ok, I'm back. I looked around the shop but was mainly looking at her. The shop was selling shirts, music, books, and Halloween style vampire merchandise. It didn't buy anything, but did try to hit on the girl. Hey, you can't fault a guy for trying right? She liked the fact that I had tattoos and she liked my "northern accent". Once the conversation turned to snakes, I needed to end it. Remember, I hate snakes.

I left the shop and went to a local diner for a burger. After dinner, I went back to the hotel to relax. I fell asleep around midnight. At two in the morning, I woke up to use the restroom. As I walked back to my bed, I thought I heard what sounded like laughing. I opened the door and looked out into the courtyard. I was looking to see if anyone else who was staying there was up. I saw all the doors closed and lights off. As I got into bed, it clicked. The fountain was right outside. Did I hear the laughs of children? I drifted off, when I heard the laughs again. This time, I could hear that they were defiantly the laughs of kids. I walked out and used my EMF detector around the fountain. I did get a few hits of 3's and 4's, but they were very sporadic.

I saw a light go on in one of the rooms. Out of that room, came the young couple from earlier. They were excited and wanted to know what I was doing. It told them that I thought I heard the kids laughing, so I was just taking some readings. They wanted to help me, but I told them that there was nothing really they could do. I know they meant well, but like I said in a previous chapter, believers can be harmful as well. When I went back to my room, I grabbed my camera and pointed it out the window and towards the fountain. All that was caught was seeing the couple walking around it a few times. No voices were caught. Although, you could hear me sawing logs if you know what I mean.

In the morning, I was at the front desk checking out, when the couple came up to me wanting to know everything. This got the attention of some of the other guests. I told them of the experiences that I had and that I took some readings to check it out. That's when a lady, who was about forty five, said that she heard the laughing too. I asked her about what time she heard it and she said about two in the morning. Well, that coincides with my "encounter". Was it the spirits of kids having fun that night? I don't know, but it was nice to know someone else had it happen to them.

I left the Andrew Jackson and made my way to the Bourbon Orleans Hotel. This was the hotel that was part of the AGS package for this trip. The outside of the hotel looks small and run down. However, once you walked through the front doors, the hotel just opens up into this luxury hotel. I lucked out because I got a room on the first floor. I found out that everyone else on this trip had rooms on the fourth and fifth floor. Also, I would like to know where the fourth and fifth floor was. From the outside, you can't see above the second floor. It must have been put together like *Tetris*.

After checking in, I made my way to my room. The moment I walked in, I changed the temp in the room to about 60 degrees. It felt so good. The outside temp was 98 degrees with 90% humidity. You could almost swim to anywhere you wanted to go. It was early afternoon, so I went for another steamy walk. I visited a history of New Orleans Museum, and visited the Jackson Square. I took pictures of numerous statues and a few girls. A cool thing was I got to see this massive paddleboat go by in the canal. Also, seeing the street performers was cool. How these people get money by just standing around still is beyond me. Funny story, I got yelled at by one of the grounds keepers at Jackson Square. I was eating a sandwich and couldn't find a garbage to throw the rest way. There were a bunch of pigeons around, so I fed the bread too them. That's when the keeper came over to me and yelled at me for feeding the birds. Little did I know, there was a sign just three feet away from me saying not to feed the birds. Oops.

I went back to the hotel to cool off. As I was walking through the lobby, I ran into Loren Hamilton fro MCGH. We said hi and talked for a bit. He told me that the group was going to meet in the lobby around six for a briefing of the weekend and general greetings. After we were done, I went to my room. I watched some tv and drank a lot of water. At six, I met with the rest of the group and with Troy. Troy gave us the rundown of what we were doing and told us the rules. Later that night, around 9pn, we were going to take a walking haunted tour of the French Quarter. After the meeting, we broke for a few hours, so I had dinner and a quick nap.

I met the group in the lobby at 8:45pm. We were introduced to our tour guide, who said that we would start the tour in the hotel. Remember what I told you about psychic? Get ready to meet some loons in this one. We went to the second floor ballroom of the hotel. We were old that a woman was killed in this room by a jealous lover. After the history lesson was over, we were told by the guide to just walk around to get a feel of the room. Ok, well Loren and I sat while the others walked. The psychic ladies went over to a wall, held hands in a line, and started to talk to the walls. Loren and I just sat back and watched this. We both kind of laughed a bit.

After about 15 minutes, the guide asked us what was felt by everyone. Most of the people said that they didn't feel anything, but the psychic ladies rang in. They said that they made contact with an evil man who was "watching" us. They said that he didn't want us there and was ready to attack. They knew this because his cold presence went through them. Well, Loren and I felt the cold presence as well. How you might be asking? Well at the time they said the presence went through them is the exact time the air conditioner kicked in. Paranormal? No, I don't think so.

The next place is the balcony outside the ballroom. Here we were told that a woman was pushed off the balcony to her death. A lot of people in the group said that they could feel like they were being pushed. The psychic ladies said that it was the "evil man" wanting to do bad things again. Ok, but here is what my explanation is. The balcony is on a decline. Meaning, it is at a downward slope away from the windows/doors. It is like that for rain run off. So, people can lose their balance real easy and it feels like being pushed. The psychic ladies didn't like my explanation. Oh well.

The rest of the night, we were taken around the French Quarter to places we didn't go into, but if we had any free time, were encouraged to do so. The guide was this woman who was mid 40's and beautiful. Oh trust me, I was looking. Nice to know where I stand doesn't it? After the tour was over, it was back to the hotel. Most of the group went to Bourbon Street, while I grabbed some soft drinks and went back to my room. I wanted to get some sleep, because we had a very long day on Saturday. I fell asleep around one in the morning, but I had some entertainment before bed. I heard a commotion outside of my room window. I drew the curtains and watched a drunk guy fight a sober guy. The fight lasted only 30 seconds. The drunk guy missed two punches, but the sober guy didn't miss his. The sober guy knocked the drunk out with one punch. The sober guy looked at me and I gave him a round of applause. He smiled and walked away. I then went to bed.

The next day, we met in the lobby at 11am. We were going to take a tour of St. Louis Cemetery #1. This is one of the most famous above ground cemeteries in the Unites States. This was one of the things I was looking most forward to. Our tour guide was a man who was in his 60's and spoke with a Creole accent. What I didn't know, we were walking the entire time. Don't these southerners know we people of the north don't handle that heat very well? Needless to say, I got a very good workout the whole weekend. Along the way, we stopped at a few places of history and other interests.

When we arrived at the cemetery, I was in awe. The mere size of this place was impressive. I have seen this cemetery on numerous television shows and a few movies and now I was here. I now know why New Orleans is sometimes called the City of the Dead. These above ground cemeteries are just like cities. Some of the tombs are massive. I also learned some a neat (well to me) fact about the tombs.

Most of the tombs have multiple "tenants". Well, when a "new tenant" is going into a tomb, they take the casket out, move the bones to the back, and the new body (in casket) goes in. Sounds like it is kind of disrespectful to the older bodies, but I guess they know what they sign up for.

We made our way through, when we came to the most famous tomb in the cemetery. The tomb of Voodoo Queen Marie LaVeau. You can tell which one is hers, because her tomb is marked up with a lot of x's. They say if you mark three x's on the tomb, make an offering, and then make a wish, she is supposed to grant your wish. I was not able to do this because the tour guide told us not to and he wouldn't leave the side of the tomb. Sucks, because I wanted to try it. We also were shown some tombs of famous people including one of my favorite actors, Nicholas Cage. I know he's not dead, but his tomb is there and ready for him.

We stopped at a few other spots on the way back to the hotel. One of the places was the Louis Armstrong Park. Louis Armstrong was one of the best jazz musicians in history. I wanted to take a picture of the Armstrong statue for my dad. However, I couldn't due to it having the bird poop cleaned off of it. One of the other places of interest was one of the first recording studios in New Orleans. It is now a Laundromat, but some of the old records and some of the old recording equipment can still be seen in the establishment. The walking tour took about 4 hours and needless to say, I was tired.

We got back to the hotel around 3 in the afternoon. I grabbed a quick lunch and then had a rest in my room. I watched a movie and then took a nap. At 7pm, I made the 12 block walk to Canal Street and waited for the cable car. I was kind of excited to ride one, because I never have before. I was told that once on the car, that it would be about a 2 mile ride. When I saw the bar called Beachcombers, that's when I needed to pull the stop cable. Well, I rode the car and saw Beachcombers. I pulled the cable, but we kept going. I got a little confused, so I pulled it again. Still we kept going. Then, we slowed down and stopped at the end of the line. Turns out, that was the last stop.

The car stopped in the middle of 3 big above ground cemeteries. I was again in awe of what was around me. It was about a three block walk to Beachcombers. This is where Troy Taylor wanted us to meet before going to the mortuary for the investigation. I had a few soft drinks while checking out the bar maid. She was smoking hot. Over the next hour, everyone on the investigation came into the bar. We talked for a bit and then walked to the mortuary. We stood outside taking pictures and looking at the cemeteries. After about 20 minutes, we were allowed inside the mortuary. We were taken to a second floor viewing room, which is now a small auditorium.

We were introduced to the local paranormal group that is in charge to the mortuary. They gave us an information form to fill out and gave us rules to follow. The advice that they gave us was to not rely on video or audio evidence, but to concentrate on our feelings. Yeah, not for a scientific investigator. Also, we were told that the mortuary is used as a haunted attracting during the Halloween season. The main guy said that there were some props set up, but that they were all in the basement. Ok, this puts up a major red flag for me. If there were things set up in the basement, why wouldn't there be anything set up elsewhere? Anything that I caught, I would have to really dissect.

I recorded some audio in most of the rooms. I did not catch anything. Also, I recorded about 4 hours of video. I looked at all the set up Halloween stuff in the basement and cracked a few jokes. Around one in the morning, most of the other investigators had gone. Loren, a couple from Indiana, and I gathered in a room on the second floor. This was called the séance room, because psychics used it to communicate with the dead in the 1920's. I had one weird personal experience happen that everyone else in the room witnessed. As we sat at the table, I asked for any spirit present to make its presence known. At that time, the door to the room shook. Loren got up, opened the door, and looked out into the hall. He saw no one. Not sure of what to make of this. It was weird that the door shook the moment I asked for a sign.

The only other thing I had happen was one EVP that was caught on the second floor. I was doing some filming and had set the camera down. I could hear some people to my right talking about drinking and partying in New Orleans. When one of the ladies asked someone else in the group, "what is your favorite part of New Orleans". You can hear the other ladies in the group say Bourbon Street. However, there is another voice on the tape as well. It has an electronic wave to it and it said "it is my home". That is all that happened in the mortuary. The time was 2 in the morning when we left the mortuary. When I say we, I mean me and the Indiana couple. We waited for over an hour at the cable car stop. We got tired of waiting, so we started to walk back to Beachcombers to call a taxi. Fortunately for us, a taxi drove by as we walked.

This was my very first cab ride ever. This cab driver knew the way back, because we were back at the hotel in no time. I grabbed one more soft drink and then went to bed. In the morning, I checked out of the hotel and said goodbye to Loren and the rest. I went across the street and back into the Vampire Boutique. I bought a few shirts for friends and gave the goth chick my card. Doesn't hurt to try remember. After that, it was off to the airport. My flight was delayed for about an hour due to a mini hurricane that came through. I say mini because it was a torrential down pour and there was winds of 50 miles per hour. It was one of the coolest things I've seen.

I was sad to leave New Orleans. I was only there for 3 days, but I had a blast. Even though it was very hot and humid, it was a place that I want to go back to again. Not just for haunted things, but to visit some of the other historical buildings. If you have never been to New Orleans, I highly recommend that you do. If you don't have fun, then you suck.

CHAPTER 21:
FINAL THOUGHTS AND HINTS

I am going to close with some helpful tips if you are thinking about starting your own group. After doing this for a while, I have gotten the feel of how a basic investigation should be done. Now my group has added certain things and quirks of their own that has made us a solid group. What's good for us may not be good for others. Every team is different. You need to find what is best for you and our team. The only way to do that is to go out and investigate. These tips and thoughts will just be guidelines for you to use.

First, make sure that this is something that you want to do. It's not all the coolness and glamour that you see on television. There is a lot more that goes into an investigation than just showing up. You have to make lots of phone calls, emails, and meetings before you even see the place that you are investigating. You also need to be able to handle a lot of boredom. About 90% of the time nothing will happen on an investigation. When it comes to footage review, you need to make sure that you are patient and look/listen to everything. Do not fast forward anything. If you feel yourself getting tired, take a break and come back to it later. Also, a lot of new investigators have a hard time with this, but this takes time and money to do. This is a hobby and not a job.

Second, you need to get along with your team members. Do not try to "one up" each other. Try to work as a unit. Some people will be better at certain aspects of the investigation than others. Build around the team members strengths. If someone in your team is good at getting EVP's, then that should be there job. If another is a photo expert, than their main job is to take photos. All this being said, all team members should be taught all aspects of investigation. You'll just find out who does what the best. Just remember the old Three Musketeer motto, "All for one and one for all". Even though I am the leader of BPIMN, I wouldn't be able to do anything without the rest of the team.

Third, this also coincides with part two, but you need to have good communication with your team, clients, and other groups. We are all in this together. Keep in contact with team members between investigations. See how they are doing, especially if they had a major personal experience happen to them. Always have an open ear to any problems they might be having after a case is over. Also, let your team know when you are going to be doing any freelance work with other groups. That way, you won't have members of your team think that you are turning your back on them. Also, encourage your team to do the same. This is a good thing. You can learn how other groups conduct investigations and how they handle themselves. That way, you can share with your team what you have learned (good or bad). Stay in contact with your clients if possible. I know it can be difficult with work, life, and other cases getting in the way. Don't be overbearing, but you want to follow up to see how they are doing. Ask if things have quieted down, activity picked up, or staying the same. Let them know that you care.

Fourth, be respectful and professional to your clients. You are there to do them a service. Most of the clients are normal, well mannered people who are scared or confused as to what's going on. They are contacting you for help. Your job is to assist them in finding out what is happening. The main ting that you need to do is keep them calm and put their fears at ease. You do this by performing an honest investigation. If you find a logical explanation for the activity, tell the clients. Most of the time, they will be very happy to hear it. However, if you do find evidence, you need to share it with them too. Never lie to a client.

Fifth, get an independent party to look at your potential evidence. Don't just take your video at face value. When finished reviewing the footage, pick a friend to go over it again. Make sure that it is someone that you trust, that way they will be completely honest with you. That way, if they give you some alternate explanations that you missed, you can dismiss that evidence. Remember, when in doubt, throw it out.

Sixth, be prepared to receive a lot of criticism. People are going to call you all sorts of names. You will be called stupid, fraud, trickster, emotional leech (been called that), and other names. Take these things with a grain of salt. Don't let them get to you or let them affect you investigation. Be respectful to the fact that they don't believe. We have been told our entire lives that ghosts don't exist. So people will ask you, "Why do you look for things that aren't there". Or, as my cousin likes to ask me, "Have you found Casper yet".

Let them say what they want. You are there to do a service for someone or a business. That is either to find evidence of a haunting or to find logical explanations for what is happening. Most of the critics of the paranormal have the mentality of "I won't believe it until it happens to me". That's fine to say. Do not try to win them over in an argument. Just go out there and do your job. There is an old saying in the paranormal field. To a believer, you don't need evidence. To a non believer, no evidence is good enough.

Seventh, use your brain. What do I mean by this. Like I have said many times in this book, find explanations first. Check out the electrical system (EMF meters work here). Does the place have loose floor boards, banging pipes, etc. A tip here is to look at the books the client reads and the movies they watch. If they have heavy occult or paranormal stuff, then they might be pulling something on you. Or, others have had this happen, they are looking for attention. I learned a very helpful tip from the TAPS team. If you go into the house or business looking for a ghost, then no matter what happens, you will think it's paranormal. You don't want that. You want to go in ready to disprove things. Then, after you are done disproving, then what is left over could be paranormal. That is what I mean by using your brain.

Lastly, have fun doing this. You are going to get a rush conducting investigations, because you are looking for things that go "bump in the night". Everyone has an investigator inside of them. We all want to play the amateur sleuth or want to be part of the Scooby gang. Well, this is your chance. The only problem is, it doesn't end up being old man Jenkins from the amusement park. Also, some people' sense of adventure will come out. You will see people crawling in attics, tight spaces, and doing things they wouldn't have done before. Also, don't be afraid to joke around with each other. It will help to lighten the mood if people are nervous and also helps pass the time.

BPIMN does not charge for the investigations that we do. We are here to help people put fears at ease and to bring the paranormal closer to real science. It is a very fun yet expensive hobby. So, can you do it? As long as you can be honest, professional, have a good working relationship with others, and have a basic knowledge of how cameras work, then you should have no problem conducting investigations in the paranormal. Just keep a level head.

I thank you for you time and I hope that you have learned some things. Not only about the paranormal, but of me as well. I hope you now have a better insight about ghosts and to let you know that if you need help, that there are people like me out there to assist. If you are anyone you know is experiencing possible paranormal activity, please email us at BPIMNGHOSTS@hotmail.com.

The author would like to thank the following people for allowing me to mention them in this book.

Jeff Belanger. Jeff is the creator of ghostvillage.com, the host of 30 Odd Minutes, and a paranormal investigator and author. I thank him for all of his advice and recommend all of his books.

Loren Hamilton and Kelly Davis of MCGH. I look forward to working with you again in the future.

Adam Selzer. Adam is an author, investigator, and wise cracker.

Holly & Britt Griffith and Beyond Reality Events. I have had a blast being at the events and look forward to attending more.

Troy Taylor. Troy is a paranormal author, investigator, and owner of Weird Chicago. I recommend his books and the Chicago tours.